The Kunsthistorisch

The Kunsthistorisches Museum in Vienna

Prestel Museum Guides

Prestel

Munich · Berlin · London · New York

Media Owner and Publisher
Generaldirektor Wilfried Seipel
Kunsthistorisches Museum
1010 Vienna, Burgring 5
info@khm.at
www.khm.at

Editor
Elisabeth Herrmann-Fichtenau

Photo Credits
© *Kunsthistorisches Museum, Vienna*
Management: Stefan Zeisler
Photos: Chris Mendez, Alexander Rosoli,
Andreas Uldrich
Photo Editing: Sabine Sommer
Additional Photos: Marianne Haller,
Inge Kitlitschka, Hans Kräftner

Front Cover
Kunsthistorisches Museum seen from
Maria Theresien-Platz

Back Cover
Benvenuto Cellini, Saliera

Library of Congress Control Number is
available; British Library Cataloguing-
in-Publication Data: a catalogue record
for this book is available from the British
Library; Deutsche Nationalbibliothek
holds a record of this publication in the
Deutsche Nationalbibliografie; detailed
bibliographical data can be found under:
http://dnb.ddb.de

Prestel Verlag
Königinstrasse 9, 80539 Munich
Tel. +49 (0)89 24 29 08-300
Fax +49 (0)89 24 29 08-335
www.prestel.de

Prestel Publishing Ltd.
4, Bloomsbury Place, London WC1A 2QA
Tel. +44 (0) 20 7323-5004
Fax +44 (0) 20 7636-8004

Prestel Publishing
900 Broadway, Suite 603,
New York, NY 10003
Tel. +1 (212) 995-2720
Fax +1 (212) 995-2733
www.prestel.com

Project Co-ordination: Anja Besserer in col-
laboration with Veronika Wilhelm
Translation into English:
Paul Aston, Sliema: front matter,
Kunstkammer, Picture Gallery, Coin Cabinet,
Sarah Kane, Watford: Architectural History
of the Kunsthistorisches Museum,
Egyptian and Near Eastern Collection,
Collection of Greek and Roman Antiquities
Editing: Jane Michael, Munich
Design: a.visus, Michael Hempel, Munich
Cover Design: SOFAROBOTNIK, Augsburg
& Munich
Production: Florian Tutte
Repro: Reproline Mediateam, Munich

Printed in Germany on acid-free paper.

ISBN 978-3-7913-3603-9 (German edition)
ISBN 978-3-7913-3604-6 (English edition)
ISBN 978-3-7913-3605-3 (Italian edition)
ISBN 978-3-7913-3929-0 (French edition)

Contents

Ill. on page 2:
Cupola Hall and Staircase with "Theseus" group by Antonio Canova.

Staircase with lunette
pictures by Hans Makart.

Preface

For visitors to the *Kunsthistorisches Museum* this new Prestel guidebook is a publication which is in fact long overdue. Its approximately 280 illustrations and explanatory texts provide a complete overview of the Museum's most important collections. Available in several languages, it will serve as a vade-mecum for visitors to Vienna from home and abroad. Every year, more than 600,000 people tour the main building on the Ringstrasse; seventy-five percent of them come from all the corners of the globe, representing over a hundred different nations. Like the Louvre in Paris or the Hermitage in St Petersburg, the *Kunsthistorisches Museum* is one the cultural destinations of Europe that form an absolute highpoint of a visit to the city.

Its highly individual architecture, the ornamentation of the main staircase, the great ceiling painting, and above all the unusual interior decoration of the galleries set the *Kunsthistorisches* apart from all other museums. Unlike the Hermitage or the Louvre, which were originally planned and used as palaces, it was from the very outset conceived and constructed as a museum. The building's fascinating architectural history, which is briefly outlined in this guidebook, includes many noteworthy peculiarities, one being the (originally unplanned) installation of the three papyrus-sheaf columns in the Egyptian and Near Eastern Collection. They were a gift from Ismail, Khedive of Egypt, to Emperor Franz Joseph I, who visited Egypt on the occasion of the opening of the Suez Canal. Today they are the only ancient Egyptian monuments outside Egypt that actually serve an architectonic purpose.

The recent re-installation of the Egyptian and Near Eastern Collection and the Collection of Greek and Roman Antiquities has made a visit to the Museum even more attractive. Unfortunately, at the time of the guide's going to press, the Kunstkammer (Collection of Sculpture and Decorative Arts) is still closed to the public while comprehensive reorganisation and restoration work is carried out. However, we are confident that it will once again be revealed in all its glory by the time the second edition of the guide becomes necessary (which will hopefully be soon). In the meantime, however, the most important objects in the collection are naturally also included in this publication.

But it is not only the *Kunsthistorisches Museum's* architecture with its sumptuous décor that sets it apart from most other museums; it is also and above all the unique provenance of the collections. They are characterised by the patronage and appreciation for art of the rulers of the House of Habsburg. Even today the collections still offer a wide-ranging panorama of European art and cultural history. Thus the intimate rooms of the former Royal-Imperial Coin Cabinet also accommodate the approximately 1,200-strong portrait collection of Archduke Ferdinand of Tyrol, presenting the visitor with a veritable who's who of the

Egyptian and Near Eastern Collection, Hall I, with ancient Egyptian pillars in the form of papyrus sheaves.

View from the Vestibule into the domed Cupola Hall.

Vestibule and Staircase leading to the Egyptian and Near Eastern Collection.

Collection of Greek and Roman
Antiquities, Hall XI.

most important contemporaries and
forebears of the lord of Ambras Castle.
Alongside the aforementioned collections in the mezzanine – the Egyptian
and Near Eastern Collection, the Collection of Greek and Roman Antiquities
and the currently closed Kunstkammer
– the Picture Gallery on the first floor
with over 800 paintings on display is
one of the Museum's principal attrac-
tions. It can be traced back primarily to
the art collections of Emperor Rudolf II
and Archduke Leopold Wilhelm and
manages to achieve a supreme synthesis of the highest artistic quality that
truly transports the visitor into another
world. At the heart of the collection are
the works of the Venetian Renaissance,
with famous paintings by Giorgione,
Titian, Tintoretto and Veronese, as well
as early German painting with numerous works by Dürer and the twelve magnificent paintings of Pieter Bruegel the Elder – the largest group of pictures by this
master in a museum. The Flemish High Baroque is richly represented by paintings
of Peter Paul Rubens and others. Nor should we forget, of course, the main masters of European portraiture, from Jan van Eyck to Diego Velázquez by way of
Rembrandt Harmensz van Rijn and Sir Anthony van Dyck.

Since its holdings are derived from former imperial collections, the *Kunsthistorisches Museum* must be considered not an Austrian national museum, but a
super-national 'Gesamtkunstwerk'. This publication aims to provide visitors with
information about historical and artistic connections and thereby to contribute to
a deeper understanding of these precious objects, but admittedly even a good
guidebook can never be a substitute for a visit to the museum itself. Only in front
of the original does that communion take place which will hopefully – as part of
a process of experience – lead to emotion and surprise, or at the very least to
admiration. Only then does the work of art, and with it the museum containing it,
fulfil its proper purpose.

Wilfried Seipel
Generaldirektor des Kunsthistorischen Museums

Architectural History of the Kunsthistorisches Museum

In the eighteenth century art collections in Europe were increasingly made accessible to a wider public. As early as 1750 a public show collection – the Galerie du Luxembourg – was established in Paris. By 1800 it had become the rule in Europe to open princely and royal collections to the public on a few days of the week and in fine weather. The first independent, purpose-built museum to open was the Dulwich Picture Gallery in south London, in 1817. This was followed in 1830 by the opening of the Munich Glyptothek and the Altes Museum in Berlin; and in 1836 the first visitors stepped over the threshold of the newly built Alte Pinakothek, also in Munich.

Façade overlooking Maria Theresien-Platz, "Rome" and "Florence".

In Vienna parts of the so-called Stallburg were converted for the purpose of housing the imperial picture collection in 1710–20. The collection was then transferred to the Upper Belvedere at the instigation of Maria Theresia. This corresponded with the common European practice of making inherited or newly acquired art collections in palatial buildings accessible to a growing public. At first only travelling aristocrats and academic pupils were granted access to the imperial picture gallery, but from the late eighteenth century – on payment of an entrance fee – it was also possible for the middle classes to visit the collection.

The planning process for the Vienna Ringstrasse started in 1857, thereby providing the impetus for developing the concept of presenting the imperial collections in an appropriate, independent new building using modern suspension and construction techniques. Nonetheless, another ten years would go by before the actual architectural competition was held in 1867. The entries included that of the Vienna-based architects Hansen, Löhr, Ferstel and Hasenauer. After months of deliberation, the members of the jury and the client, Emperor Franz Joseph, were

Staircase with Canova's "Theseus" group and Munkácsy's ceiling painting.

still unable to agree on one of the proposals. Karl von Hasenauer therefore encouraged the inclusion of a colleague from outside in the decision-making process. In the summer of 1868 he approached the sixty-five-year-old Gottfried Semper, who had an excellent international reputation as an architectural theorist as well as extensive experience in the building of museums and theatres. Semper initially turned the project down, but then went on – at the emperor's request – to develop Hasenauer's plans to maturity and to give them majority appeal. Hasenauer had designed two buildings – the *Kunsthistorisches Museum* (art history museum) and the Naturhistorisches Museum (natural history museum) – facing each other on the other side of the Ringstrasse, between the Hofburg and the Stallungen (imperial stables), today's Museums Quarter. Semper retained the concept, but extended it further to embrace the notion of an 'imperial forum', ultimately harking back to classical models of city planning.

In addition to the museum buildings Semper proposed symmetrically positioned structures, each with a segment-shaped porch. The Leopoldine wing of the Hofburg, which lay at right angles, was to be given a façade matching that of the new buildings as well as having a throne room added in the middle. This would have acted as a prelude to a city-wide axis via the Ringstrasse to the Hofstallungen (imperial stables). As a further component of the imperial forum Semper designed two triumphal arches, which were to span the Ringstrasse where it bisected the vast square, connecting the museums with the new buildings on the Heldenplatz.

However, the only buildings that were ever actually realised were the two museums and, facing the Burggarten to the south-east, the part of the Hofburg known as the 'Neue Burg'. In 1871 construction work began on the two museums. Twenty years later, in 1891, they were ready to open. From the start, the collaboration between Semper and Hasenauer was fraught with difficulty. Up to the time of Semper's involuntary departure from Vienna in 1876, the division of responsibilities was not regulated by contract. Despite every attempt at professionalism, the difference in age and the contrast between the Viennese Hasenauer's neo-Baroque temperament and the Hamburger Semper's down-to-earth approach made it highly improbable that they would be able complete the project jointly.

Under Semper's influence the façades of the museum Hasenauer had designed were smoothed out and overlaid with a rich artistic overall programme in which Semper's vision of art history was reflected. At ground level can be seen the various arts and crafts representing the 'material world'; on the first floor are allegories of the most important European art centres representing 'cultural historical' civilisation, and finally at the balustrade level stand figures of the most important European artists, an expression of the 'realm of the individual'. According to another, parallel, ordering principle, each of the four façades of the rectangular building is

Gottfried Semper and Karl von
Hasenauer: a bird's-eye view
of the "Kaiserforum", 1869.
(©: Österreichisches Staatsarchiv)

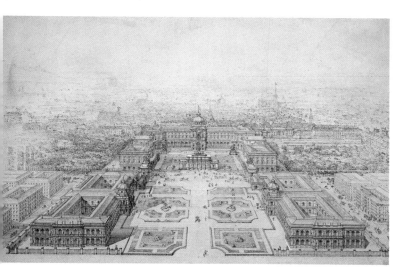

dedicated to a different period in the history of art. The figures on the façade facing Babenbergerstrasse represent antiquity; those on Lastenstrasse are from the
Middle Ages; the side facing Maria Theresien-Platz celebrates the Renaissance; and
finally that on the Burgring illustrates modern times. It is no coincidence that the
accomplishments of the Renaissance are presented in the sculptural decoration of
the main façade: indeed the architectonic design vocabulary of the entire building
is modelled on High Renaissance forms. This particular stylistic approach had its
origins in Leo von Klenze's Alte Pinakothek in Munich (1836).

The internal structure combines several building traditions: the entrance hall,
main staircase and cupola hall present a dramaturgical unity celebrating the imperial client and his predecessors. In essential points Semper and Hasenauer adapted
the decoration and conception of the staircase from the late Baroque Palazzo
Reale in Caserta (1752 onwards, architect: Luigi Vanvitelli). An additional refine-
ment is the circular cut in the ceiling of the Entrance Hall, which affords visitors a
first glimpse of the Cupola Hall (ill. p. 10) as soon as they enter the museum. Light
enters through this opening, illuminating a lobby dominated by muted colours –
an allusion to the Roman Pantheon. Walking up the Grand Staircase, best seen
when flooded with sunlight, the visitor is led past Antonio Canova's *Theseus and
the Centaur* and into the Cupola Hall, the apogee of imperial self-dramatisation.

When it came to laying out the exhibition halls the emperor – in conjunction
with his scientific court officials – turned to a model that, at least since the opening

Façade overlooking
Maria Theresien-Platz.

of the Alte Pinakothek in Munich, had become the standard: namely, the combination of large exhibition halls with a series of small side rooms. Based on a symmetrical floor plan, and divided by the central axis comprising Entrance Hall, Staircase and Cupola Hall, each group of side rooms forms a circuit around an inner courtyard, thus making it possible for visitors to follow a convenient route. In the mezzanine these great halls lie on the outer façade, the side rooms accordingly bordering the inner courtyard. Above, in the rooms of the Picture Gallery, it works the other way around: light from above streams into the great halls that face the courtyard, while the side rooms surrounding them receive the necessary light through window openings on the outside wall. In line with the state of technological development at the time it was built, the entire building was designed and used as a daylight museum. At dusk, therefore, the galleries had to be closed.

The original installation of the different collections can be appreciated in the high-quality and academically ambitious decoration of the rooms. In the mezzanine the following collections were accommodated one after the other: the 'Egyptian Antiquities' (today: Egyptian and Near Eastern Collection); the 'Classical Antiquities' (today: Collection of Greek and Roman Antiquities); the 'Collection of Coins and Medals' (today: Coin Cabinet, second floor); the 'Collection of Art-Industry Objects from the Middle Ages and Modern Times (today: Kunstkammer); and finally the 'Weapons Collection' (today: Collection of Arms and Armour, since 1935 in the Neue Burg). Fundamentally, the architects chose as the guiding decorative principle for the ceilings delicate Renaissance structural features, in which references were made to the objects displayed beneath. This pattern is interrupted in the rooms of the Egyptian and Near Eastern Collection, the central hall of the Collection of Greek and Roman Antiquities and the large hall of the Kunstkammer (Collection of Sculpture and Decorative Arts). In the Egyptian halls, ancient papyrus-sheaf columns support the walls of the Picture Gallery above; wall paintings, door jambs and display cabinets borrow Egyptian motifs. Such a comprehensive adaptation of museum rooms to the content of the displays had previously been achieved in Berlin's Neues Museum, opened in 1850 (architect: August Stüler). The central hall of the Collection of Greek and Roman Antiquities incorporates late Roman barrel vaulting, while the picture frieze running round the gallery presents the twelve most important Greco-Roman gods.

Finally, in the late Baroque hall of the Kunstkammer (the Collection of Sculpture and Decorative Arts), a large ceiling painting celebrates the *Patrons of the Visual Arts in the House of Habsburg*. Logically, this hall lies in the main representational axis consisting of Entrance Hall / Main Staircase / Cupola Hall, and it is here that two key ideas are bound up with one another in a sophisticated way: Habsburg self-representation and space for the academically arranged collection. On the central

Staircase with lunette, spandrel and intercolumnar pictures by Hans Makart and Gustav Klimt.

axis Baroque-style decorative elements are densely packed into what is certainly one of the most exuberant and costly interior spaces of Viennese late historicism, if not the whole of European museum architecture. The overall impression is dominated by the polychromy of marble and *stucco lustro* and the ceiling and wall paintings in the staircase, executed by famous artists including Mihály von Munkácsy (ceiling paintings), Hans Makart (lunettes) and Gustav Klimt (spandrels opposite the Cupola Hall). The rich relief decoration of the Cupola Hall includes portrait medallions of the emperors Maximilian I, Charles V, Rudolf II, the archdukes Ferdinand (II), Albrecht (VII) and Leopold Wilhelm, as well as the emperors Charles VI and Franz Joseph I by Johann Benk; the reliefs are by Rudoph Weyr. By contrast, the rooms of the Picture Gallery are decorated only in the ceiling area with monochrome stucco adornments punctuated by gold highlights. The proportion of the top-lit rooms – in other words the relationship between the size of the room and the height of the ceiling – ensured in times of pure daylight illumination an optimal angle of incidence and therefore the greatest possible surface area for the hanging of paintings.

Much of the above description also holds true for the Naturhistorisches Museum on the opposite side of Maria Theresien-Platz. The basic disposition of the rooms is the same, and the decorative programme is equally attuned to the collections, but in line with its more down-to-earth subject matter, those responsible for the interior decoration of this building avoided the same all-pervasive polychrome backdrops, the prolific wall decorations and the dominant imperial presence.

Egyptian and Near Eastern Collection

Ill. on pages 20/21:
Hall I of the Egyptian and
Near Eastern Collection.

Thanks to its exceptionally rich holdings of monuments from the Old Kingdom, the Egyptian and Near Eastern Collection of the *Kunsthistorisches Museum* ranks among the greatest collections of its kind. It largely came into being in the nineteenth and twentieth centuries and is composed of purchases, gifts and new acquisitions from excavations.

The few Egyptian antiquities that already belonged to the Habsburgs in the eighteenth century were recorded in the cabinet of coins and antiquities. A certain 'emancipation' occurred only at the start of the nineteenth century when, in the wake of Napoleon's sensational campaign in Egypt (1798–1799), Egyptian culture came to be esteemed as never before. The collection grew steadily thanks to famous donations. Its greatest expansion took place in 1821 with a generous purchase in Egypt, which increased the size of its holdings to several thousand objects. On account of this growth and the consequent shortage of space, it soon became necessary to find new premises for the collection, which up until then had been housed together with the collection of classical antiquities in the Augustinergang behind the Hofbibliothek (Imperial Library). In 1824 the collection opened to the public in a grand house on Johannesgasse, but this independent existence was not to last. In 1837 it had to move into the Lower Belvedere, already home to the collection of classical antiquities. The most important donations were made around the mid-century by Anton Ritter von Laurin, Austrian consul general in Alexandria from 1824 to 1849, who was also responsible for the discovery of the splendid stone sarcophagus of Nes-shu-tefnu. Finally, in 1878, the collection grew substantially thanks to the inclusion of the Miramar collection of Archduke Ferdinand Max, later Emperor Maximilian of Mexico, who was executed in 1867. But it was only with the opening of the *Kunsthistorisches Museum* – which was to be a compendium of all the Habsburg art collections – that the Egyptian Collection was allocated its own suite of rooms.

In the twentieth century the majority of new acquisitions came about through Austrian excavations in Egypt. Of particular importance were the excavations carried out by Hermann Junker between 1912 and 1929 in the pyramid complex of Giza, to which we owe almost the entire wealth of monuments from the third millennium BC (Old Kingdom), among them the famous *Reserve Head,* numerous funerary statues, inscribed and painted architectural fragments such as false doors and architraves, stone and wood coffins, canopies, jewellery and vessels made out of different materials. In 1913, private funds enabled the purchase of the cult chamber of Ka-ni-nisut, which at that time was in the possession of the Egyptian Antiquities Service.

Monuments from the ancient culture of South Arabia are key features of the Near Eastern collection. The core of the collection owes its existence to Eduard

Ernst Weidenbach, Catching Birds,
Hall I.

Glaser (died 1908), who undertook four research trips to the Yemen between 1882 and 1895. The South Arabian epigraphs collected by him are even today of fundamental importance for the study of ancient Yemen.

The galleries displaying the Egyptian and Near Eastern Collection are impressive on account of their grandiose furnishings. The Egyptian-inspired decoration of the ceilings and corridors, the display cases and other fittings were part of the original plan of the architects Gottfried Semper and Karl von Hasenauer. Unlike the remaining halls in the mezzanine, which retain their ribbed vaults and Renaissance décor, each of the Egyptian halls has – apart from its ancient Egyptian décor – barrel vaulting. Uniquely, three original Egyptian monolithic pillars over six metres in height are reused in two halls to support the ceiling in place of the marble columns of the other halls. Emperor Franz Joseph I was given them as a gift when he travelled to Egypt in 1869 to attend the opening of the Suez Canal. Of particular note are the wall paintings (on paper) in Hall I, which lend a special character to this large gallery. They are copies of wall paintings from the grave of Prince Chnum-hetep in Beni Hassan in Middle Egypt that Ernst Weidenbach created for the Vienna World's Fair of 1874. For reasons of space it was not possible to produce a copy of the tomb in the museum, but none of the important scenes is missing: the offering scene, bird hunting and sea jousting, depictions of craftsmen, fishermen, shepherds and huntsmen.

For many years the reorganisation of the display rooms of the Egyptian and Near Eastern Collection was a major desideratum. On the one hand the rooms urgently needed structural renovation and on the other hand vital technical equipment was lacking. In 2001, however, the collection was finally reopened with great fanfare. In the meantime it had acquired an additional room (Hall IX), with a glazed pyramid at the centre, so that today the collection has five large halls and five side rooms at its disposal.

Following new curatorial principles, the collection is now divided into four areas, beginning with the cult of the dead in Halls I, II, III and V. In addition to numerous sarcophagi, human and animal mummies, books of the dead, funerary stelae and figures of gods, a particular highlight is the Old Kingdom offering chamber of Ka-ni-nisut, which is richly decorated with relief representations. The second subject area concerns the cultural history of Egypt, with Halls IV and VI displaying objects connected with religion and daily life such as clothing, tools, containers, jewellery and cosmetics. Halls VII, VIII and IX – the next section of the collection – are devoted to the visual arts, in particular sculpture in the round. The *Reserve Head* from the pyramid complex of Giza, dating from the Fourth Dynasty, is an especially fine example. Finally, Hall VIa documents the development of ancient Egyptian writing and its decoding, as well as cuneiform, which was used for various languages in the lands of the Near East. Also on show in this room are objects from the ancient South Arabia collection, such as portrait stelae, small reliefs and monumental building inscriptions. Babylon is represented by the depiction of a lion made of glazed bricks from the Ishtar Gate.

OFFERING CHAMBER OF KA-NI-NISUT

Early Fifth Dynasty, *c.* 2450 BC
From the Giza pyramid complex
Limestone, width 370 cm, depth 150 cm
Inv. No. ÄS 8006

The south end of the mastaba of the royal official Ka-ni-nisut was widened to allow for the construction of an offering chamber: an overground room where offerings for the dead were regularly made by relatives, or rather mortuary priests. The southernmost false door is the main cult place, forming the connection between this life and the next and enabling Ka-ni-nisut symbolically to receive the offerings.

The reliefs refer to the actions of those bearing gifts; they depict scenes of slaughter and the great offering lists.

Ka-ni-nisut is shown in his chancellery with rows of scribes as well as with his wife and three children. Sailing and rowing boots are necessary for the journey to Abydos, the place of worship of the god Osiris.

RESERVE HEAD

Old Kingdom, Fourth Dynasty,
Cheops (2609–2584 BC)
From Giza, cemetery west of the Cheops pyramid
Limestone, height 27.7 cm, width 17.3 cm, depth 24.5 cm
Inv. No. ÄS 7787

The portrait- or reserve head is one of the key works in the collection. It was found in one of the early mastaba tombs in the Giza necropolis in front of the underground burial chamber. Of the thirty-three such heads known today, the Viennese example is the finest. In spite of its idealised, regular and clear features, the face offers a life-like portrait. According to the traditional view, at a time when mummification techniques had not yet been perfected, these sculptures were 'surrogate heads' for the souls of the dead. Deliberate damage could be attributable to the magic function of these heads.

CHENT AND HER SON RUDJU

Old Kingdom, first half of the Fifth Dynasty,
C. 2450 BC
From Giza, cemetery west of the Cheops
pyramid
Limestone, height 53 cm, width 26 cm,
depth 38 cm
Inv. No. ÄS 7507

Funerary statues were placed in an inaccessible room of the mastaba, the so-called *serdab*. They were meant to take part, as a kind of second self, in the funerary rituals that were being performed in the adjoining offering chamber in front of the false door. Chent (full name Chentkai) was the wife of a high-ranking official. What is noteworthy about this sculpture is that her own hair is visible on her forehead under her wig. Her son Rudju is represented as a small child.

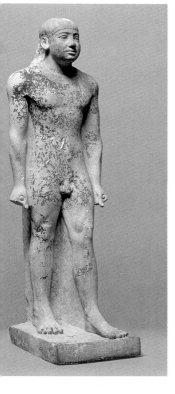

SNOFRU-NEFER
Old Kingdom, late Fifth Dynasty, c. 2400 BC
From Giza, cemetery west of the Cheops
pyramid
Limestone, height 78 cm, width 23.7 cm,
depth 28.5 cm
Inv. No. ÄS 7506

KAI-PU-PTAH AND IPEP
Old Kingdom, late Fifth Dynasty, c. 2400 BC
From Giza, cemetery west of the Cheops
pyramid
Limestone, height 56 cm, width 28 cm,
depth 22.3 cm
Inv. No. ÄS 7444

This statue of the 'inspector of court
singers' and 'director of entertainment'
Snofru-nefer comes from his grave.
It is one of the rare depictions of a naked,
standing young man from the Old
Kingdom and could be interpreted as
an expression of certain aspects of the
Egyptians' beliefs about death, such as
'vitality' or 'rejuvenation'. The statue
embodies the very highest ideals of
Egyptian art – in particular sculpture in
the round – namely immobility, symmetry, solidity, frontality and idealisation.

Funerary statues of a man and a woman.
The gesture of the woman, passing her
right arm round the back of the man,
while her left arm rests on his left arm –
is the conventional expression for the
bond of love. The man is wearing a
round curly-haired wig and a short,
smooth kilt, the woman a shoulder-
length striated wig and the usual long,
tight-fitting dress.

BA-BA-EF

Old Kingdom, beginning of the Fifth Dynasty,
C. 2450 BC
From Giza, cemetery west of the Cheops
pyramid
Calcite ("alabaster"), height 49.7 cm,
width 16.3 cm, depth 22.5 cm
Inv. No. ÄS 7785

Funerary statue of a high-ranking official
with 'gala kilt', the right-hand section
of which is pleated. Ba-ba-ef's gaze is
clearly directed upwards. Characteristic
of the Old Kingdom representation of
the human form is the athletic stance,
as demonstrated especially in the broad,
bulky shoulders, muscular limbs and
upright bearing.

TOMB RELIEF OF CHETI

Middle Kingdom, early Twelfth Dynasty,
C. 1980 BC
Origin unknown
Limestone, height 44 cm, width 77.2 cm,
depth 11.2 cm
Inv. No. ÄS 202

The Old Kingdom was followed by a
period of political and economic decline.
After the kings of the late Eleventh
Dynasty had reunited the kingdom, a
difficult process of consolidation ensued.
This development is also reflected in the
visual arts: in the First Intermediate Period
the classical style was abandoned, only
to be gradually reintroduced in the early
Middle Kingdom. The relief of Cheti,
while still exhibiting some of the stylistic
features of the turbulent period that preceded it, is nevertheless already executed
according to the new proportional grid,
which is still visible as an underdrawing.
Of particular appeal is the seemingly
naive arrangement together with the
meticulous rendering of details and the
very well-preserved colour scheme.
The theme of the relief is a man and a
woman receiving from their son tomb
fittings and a rich offering for the dead.

SPHINX HEAD OF SESOSTRIS III

Middle Kingdom, Twelfth Dynasty,
Sesostris III (1878–1843 BC)
Origin unknown
Siltstone, height 21.9 cm, width 33.2 cm,
depth 32.1 cm
Inv. No. ÄS 5813

The Twelfth Dynasty (c. 1990–1785 BC)
was the core period of the Middle Kingdom. Its founder, Amenemhat I, vizier to
the last Mentuhotep (Eleventh Dynasty),
had usurped the throne. His principal
concerns were the unification of the two
halves of the country (Upper and Lower
Egypt), which in the preceding First Intermediate Period had developed indepen-
dently of one another, and the chan-
nelling of disparate spiritual movements.
Amenemhat's successors were similarly

preoccupied with the strengthening of the king's power and the attainment of political absolutism. Under Sesostris III and his son Amenemhat III this aspiration was expressed in the style of royal sculpture, which came to be characterised by realistic, serious, hard features. This impressive king's head has been identified with Sesostris III on stylistic grounds and represents one of the most magnificent portraits of this ruler. The form of the headdress and the details of the break – which are most clearly visible in the side view – show that the head was once part not of a human-figure statue but of the leonine body of a sphinx.

SEBEK-EM-SAF

Middle Kingdom, probably Thirteenth
Dynasty, c. 1700 BC
Probably from Armant
Granodiorite, height 150 cm, width 43 cm,
depth 61.5 cm
Inv. Nos. ÄS 5051, ÄS 5801

This is one of the most magnificent
non-royal statues from a time that is
already clearly marked by the decline
that preceded the reign of the Hyksos.
The subject, particularly striking for his
corpulence, was an important figure.
Both his father – a high-ranking official –
and his sister, who was the wife of a
king, are depicted in several monuments.
Sebek-em-saf is bald, his dress consisting
of an ankle-length kilt knotted under the
chest.

SHRINE OF HORI
Middle Kingdom, late Twelfth
or Thirteenth Dynasty,
C. 1800–1700 BC
Probably from Abydos
limestone, height 49 cm,
width 39 cm, depth 25.5 cm
Inv. No. ÄS 186

The construction of the upper side of this cuboid block indicates a barrel vault with raised end walls, an ancient form of sacred architecture. On the front a niche has been added, in which the figure of a sitting man is visible in semi-relief. All four sides of the monument bear inscriptions. From these we learn that the shrine was erected in Abydos as a cenotaph, so that Hori and his numerous relatives could take part in the worship and mysteries of Osiris.

HIPPOPOTAMUS
Middle Kingdom, Eleventh/Twelfth Dynasty,
C. 2000 BC
From Dra Abu-el-Naga
Faience, height 11 cm, length 20.5 cm,
width 7.65 cm
Inv. No. ÄS 4211

In the Middle Kingdom small hippopotamus figures such as this one served as grave goods. Hippopotamus hunting was a privilege bestowed by the king on private individuals. The animal's habitat (papyrus, lotus, a bird) is painted on its body, giving the impression that the hippo is walking through the dense vegetation of a swamp.

KING THUTMOSIS III

New Kingdom, Eighteenth Dynasty,
Thutmosis III (1504–1452 BC)
Origin unknown, possibly from Thebes
Granodorite, height 46.5 cm,
width 30.6 cm, depth 20.3 cm
Inv. No. ÄS 70

Royal portrait with headdress, uraeus snake and wide ritual beard; naked upper body. If this were a standing, not a kneeling figure, it would originally have reached a height of just under 1.2 metres. The fine features with the angular profile and the hooked nose indicate the person of King Thutmosis III, the great conqueror under whom the Egyptian sphere of influence reached its greatest ever extent, stretching from Syria in the north down to the Fourth Nile Cataract in present-day Sudan.

TJENENA

New Kingdom, Eighteenth Dynasty,
Thutmosis IV, c. 1410 BC
Origin unknown, possibly from Thebes
Limestone, height 56 cm, width 15.8 cm,
depth 35.7 cm
Inv. No. ÄS 63

This meticulously painted seated statue of a senior official depicts a man with a striated wig, short chin beard and a long cloak that covers his left shoulder. The seat back is in the form of a rounded stela. The inscription on the reverse of the seat has been partially hacked away, while that on the sides of the pedestal has completely disappeared. Similar damage has been done to the inscriptions and images of the Theban tomb from which this statue is supposed to have come, indicating that the royal fan-bearer had already fallen from grace in his own lifetime.

HAMADRYAS BABOON
New Kingdom, Eighteenth Dynasty,
Amenophis III, 1410–1372 BC
Origin unknown, probably from Thebes
Red granite, height 130 cm, width 42 cm,
depth 61.5 cm
Inv. No. ÄS 5782

The noisy 'whooping' of the Hamadryas baboon at sunrise and sunset in its rocky habitat served as the perfect example for greeting and bidding farewell to the sun at the critical points of its cycle; with their raised hands in the typical Egyptian gesture of adoration these animals became a symbol of this endlessly recurring process. In the books of the dead, baboons embody the 'eastern souls', in other words the gods that cheer the sun as it comes up over the horizon. They are joined by the king in his role as sun priest.

GODDESS SACHMET
New Kingdom,
Eighteenth Dynasty,
Amenophis III (1410–1372 BC
Probably from the Mut
temple in Karnak, Thebes
Granodorite, height 197 cm,
width 45.9 cm, depth 101.7 c
(reconstructed)
Inv. No. ÄS 77

This goddess, who is represented with the head of a lioness and whose name means 'The Mighty One', has a predominantly wild and dangerous character, which is mainly deployed, however, in the defence of the king. In the Mut Temple at Karnak Amenophis III erected a vast memorial to her in the form of around 600 colossal statues. We should certainly therefore see in this statue evidence for the conflation of the two goddesses Mut and Sachmet, who belong to the triads of the twin capital cities of Thebes and Memphis. The Vienna collection owns in total five such seated statues. Two of them were already in the collection by 1818.

TOMB RELIEF OF
THE ROYAL TUTOR MERI-RE

Eighteenth Dynasty,
Amenophis III (1410–1372 BC)
From Sakkara
Painted limestone, height 130.2 cm,
width 87 cm
Inv. No. ÄS 5814

The glittering reign of Amenophis III is reflected in the style of the visual arts of the period. Great care was exercised in the depiction of fashionable clothing, wigs and jewellery.
In the upper register Meri-re and his wife Baket-amun come to worship the god Re-Harachti-Amun, as is recorded in the inscription. Below the couple is presented with a bouquet of flowers by their son. Meri-re holds a fruit to the mouth of Prince Satem, who is sitting on his lap – a vehicle for expressing the title 'Royal Tutor'.

CROUCHING STATUE OF
CHAI-HAPI

New Kingdom, probably second half of the Nineteenth Dynasty, c. 1250–1200 BC
Probably from Heliopolis
Gneiss, height 49.5 cm, width 19.8 cm, depth 31.4 cm
Inv. No. ÄS 64

The small crouching statue, which was excavated in Vienna around 1800 together with Roman finds, may come from a shrine to the cult of Serapis or Isis. Judging by the style and inscriptions, however, it would originally have stood, almost 1,500 years earlier, in a temple at Heliopolis.
Chai-hapi holds in front of him a stylised sistrum (rattle), on which the face of the goddess Hathor (with cow ears) is depicted.

THE GOD IMI-CHENT-WER

Possibly New Kingdom, Nineteenth Dynasty, Ramses II (1304–1237 BC) or later
Probably from the area around Memphis
Siltstone, height 115 cm, width 50 cm, depth 36 cm
Inv. No. ÄS 5770

Standing figure with wig, wide plaited beard typical of the gods, wide pearl collar and pleated, short god's kilt; the upper body is naked. Written in large hieroglyphics on the back pillar is the name of the god (about whom very little else is known), as well as the start of the first of the two cartouche names of the royal donor, User-maat-re – insufficient evidence, unfortunately, to allow an unequivocal identification with a definite personality. The sculpture is also hard to evaluate from a stylistic point of view. Moreover, the upper part of the forehead has been reworked and even the inscription may be of a later date.

GEM-NEF-HOR-BAK

Late Period, Thirtieth Dynasty, first half of the fourth century BC
Probably from Sais
Granodorite, height 51 cm, width 18 cm, depth 25.5 cm
Inv. No. ÄS 62

Records show that this statue was the very first piece to enter the Vienna Collection of Egyptian and Near Eastern Antiquities. It was acquired in Constantinople around 1560, having possibly been brought there in imperial Roman times. Gem-nef-hor-bak is wearing the pouch-shaped wig that is usual for the Late Period; he appears to be naked, kneeling and without jewellery and holds a small naos (shrine) in front of him, in which a figure of the goddess Neith is standing. The texts on the sides of the shrine extol the goddess, while the inscription on the back pillar carries tributes to Gem-nef-hor-bak.

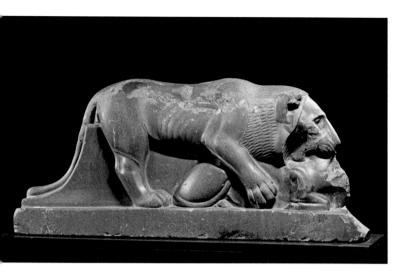

LION DEVOURING A BULL

Thirtieth Dynasty, middle of the
fourth century BC (?)
Origin unknown
Siltstone, height 28 cm, length 61.5 cm,
width 13 cm
Inv. No. ÄS 8020

This thematically unique sculpture
shows a lion gripping a bull (depicted
on a smaller scale), whose head he is in
the process of devouring. This sculptural group could be represent the idol of
the lion god Miysis, the principal god of
Leontopolis in the East Delta, that was
hidden in the temple's holy of holies.

HEAD OF AN OLD MAN

Ptolemaic Period, c. third century BC
Origin unknown
Siltstone, height 31.3 cm, width 15 cm,
depth 14.5 cm
Inv. No. ÄS 42

Deriving from a somewhat larger-than-
life statue, this portrait head of an
important personage fascinates us on
account of its marked realism, which
comes across despite the idealised
means of representation. What stands
out is the smooth, pouch-shaped wig,
which is typical of idealised heads from
the Late Period to the Ptolemaic period.
This head is one of the finest examples of
the successful synthesis of Egyptian and
Hellenistic art.

**MUMMY-SHAPED INNER COFFIN
OF PA-DI-ASET**
Twenty-fifth/Twenty-sixth Dynasty,
C. 660 BC
From Achmim
Wood with cartonnage, painted,
length 183 cm, width 44 cm, depth 35 cm
Inv. No. ÄS 8902

The associated outer coffin and the
mummy are preserved. The images on
the lid show the Abydos fetish (Abydos
being the mythical burial place of Osiris),
the presentation of Pa-di-aset before
Osiris, the weighing of souls, the mummy
on a bier and the adoration of Osiris in
the tree. As the god of resurrection,
Osiris is also god of vegetation – the
generator of new life.

SARCOPHAGUS OF PA-NEHEM-ISIS

Ptolemaic period, second century BC
From Sakkara
Greywacke, length 205 cm, width 66.5 cm,
depth 47.5 cm
Inv. No. ÄS 4

The hard stone has been polished and engraved with great care. The finely napped surface of the figurative elements provides a strong contrast to smooth surrounding surfaces. The jewelled collar appears small and unimportant.

What dominates instead are the representations of gods of the netherworld, the worship of the sun, the Ba-bird and the mummy on the bier. On the back of the head Isis and Nephthys can be seen embracing the Abydos fetish. The long inscriptions contain netherworld texts and an idealised biography.

Collection of Greek and Roman Antiquities

The high status which antiquity is accorded in the *Kunsthistorisches Museum* forms as it were the spiritual foundation of the collections. Even the external appearance of the building announces the fact: a bronze statue of Pallas Athene, goddess of wisdom and patroness of science and art, crowns the museum's cupola and is clearly visible from afar.

The *Kunsthistorisches Museum's* Collection of Greek and Roman Antiquities is one of the most important of its kind in the world. Its holdings span a time frame of more than three thousand years and extend from Bronze Age Cypriot pottery of the third millennium BC right up to the medieval finds of the eleventh to the thirteenth centuries AD. Of the very greatest art- and cultural historical value are the unique cameos as well as the treasures from the time of the Great Migration and the early Middle Ages.

Historically speaking, it is significant that the collection originally formed part of the Habsburg possessions. Works of antiquity were collected at the Viennese court at least from the sixteenth century, with the result that many outstanding pieces had already been acquired at an early stage: the exquisite *Gemma Augustea* under Rudolf II (reigned 1576–1612); the *Sarcophagus with Fighting Amazons* in the seventeenth century; and the *Senatus Consultum de Bacchanalibus* under Charles VI (reigned 1711–1740).

During the eighteenth century, the archaeological excavations of the cities surrounding Vesuvius, together with German Classicism, revived interest in Greek and Roman antiquity, triggering off a collecting fever that produced astonishing results. From all parts of the empire, archaeological finds flowed into the imperial collection in Vienna. Some were acquired in a more or less haphazard fashion, but others came specifically from excavations or were acquired on journeys. The discovery of the most important hoards from the eastern part of the empire – including that unearthed in 1799 in Nagyszentmiklós – can be seen as a stroke of good fortune; nonetheless, the way these disparate pieces were then drawn together in the ambit of the court was highly methodical. As early as 1779, Maria Theresia transferred the carved stones – among them the valuable cameos – from the Schatzkammer (the imperial treasury) to the Coin Cabinet, which since 1765 had been housed in a part of the Hofburg palace known as the Augustinergang.

1798 can be considered as the year in which the Collection of Greek and Roman Antiquities formally came into being, for it was in that year that Franz de Paula Neumann was appointed sole director of the now united 'Imperial Cabinet of Coins and Classical Antiquities'. During his period in office (1798–1816) he worked single-mindedly towards the establishment of a comprehensive cabinet of Greek and Roman antiquities. As well as gems and precious items, it was intended

Hall XI with the Sarcophagus with Fighting Amazons.

Roman portrait gallery in Hall XIII.

to reflect as extensively as possible the material legacy of antiquity. Stone sculptures, busts and bronzes, which up until then had been treated as individual pieces serving first and foremost as decoration for state rooms and gardens, were brought together from the various imperial residences, in other words from the Schatzkammer (Treasury), from Schönbrunn Palace and from the Belvedere.

The collection was enriched above all by purchases from private collections, mostly for very considerable sums, which laid the foundations for the holdings of ancient vases and bronzes. In 1802 in Rome and Naples, the painter Michael Wutky bought a large number of Greek and Roman antiquities to the value of more than 9,000 guilders on behalf of the imperial collection; in 1804 sculptures, vases and bronzes from the collection of Vincenz Maria von Rainer zu Harbach were purchased against a life annuity of 2,500 guilders; 30,000 guilders were spent in 1808 on numerous pieces from the estate of Angelo de France; and in 1815 no less than 125,000 guilders were paid out for the comprehensive collection of sculptures and over 600 vases that had belonged to Count Anton von Lamberg-Sprinzenstein. This was the last time that such large amounts of money were available, marking the end of the systematic building up of the collection.

The Augustinergang was soon bursting at the seams with treasures. In 1823, in order to relieve the pressure, a great number of Roman antiquities were placed in the underground rooms of the Temple of Theseus in the Volksgarten, which were also open to the public. It was not long, however, before these rooms had to be closed on account of the prevailing dampness. In 1845 all the ancient sculptures and stone inscriptions were transferred to the Lower Belvedere. Apart from individual acquisitions, donations and bequests, which occurred at regular intervals, the collection experienced several periods of significant growth during the second half of the nineteenth century. The sculpture and architecture holdings in particular were substantially enlarged as a result of Austria's archaeological projects in Eastern Greece and Asia Minor (1873 and 1875 in Samothrace, 1882–1884

Sculpture in Hall X
with the ceiling painting
by Franz Xaver Simm:
"Archaeology".

Hall XVIII with the Bust of Eutropios.

in Trysa and 1895–1906 in Ephesus); in 1880 the classical antiquities of the Ambras Collection were absorbed, as were those of the Este-Catajo Collection in 1923. In 1940 the collection of Greek vases was enriched with a number of precious pieces through the integration of antiquities from the former Austrian Museum for Art and Industry.

In 1891, the Collection of Greek and Roman Antiquities was moved from the Augustinergang and the Lower Belvedere into the newly opened *Kunsthistorisches Museum*; in 1900 the coin collections were separated from the classical antiquities collection. There was insufficient space in the galleries, however, for the finds from Ephesus and Samothrace, or for the Heroon of Trysa reliefs. In 1978, after a series of temporary arrangements, the Ephesus Museum was finally ready to open in the Neue Burg, but to this day no permanent location has been found for the proper display of the *Heroon of Trysa* reliefs.

Urgently needed construction and general redevelopment works, especially the complete electrification of all the exhibition rooms, as well as the long-awaited updating of the displays, forced the collection to close for a long period of time. When it re-opened in 2005 it was not only presented in a new light, but had also expanded into nine halls and seven side rooms with a total floor area of 1,452 m². Compared with the old installation the number of exhibits has now risen by a third to around 2,500 objects. The overall concept of the new installation is characterised to a lesser extent by different material groups, but now takes much more account of cultural-historical connections and educational interest. Thus, for example, the development of the Roman portrait is illustrated for the first time in its own portrait gallery, and core themes are set out in the new side rooms: the culture and art of Cyprus, Etruria and Lower Italy as well as Roman Austria.

**VOTIVE STATUE OF
A MAN**
Cypro-Archaic,
second half of the sixth
century BC
From Pyla (Cyprus)
Limestone, height 201 cm
Inv. No. ANSA I 341

This larger-than-life-size statue of a priest was found in a shrine near Pyla on the island of Cyprus. The head is crowned with a wreath of leaves and is dominated by the almond-shaped eyes and rigidly geometrical curls of the beard. The priest is wearing a cloak on which traces of red paint are visible. The almost unflinching stance, as well as the proportions of the statue, are typical of large-scale Archaic Greek sculpture. Furthermore, Egyptian influences – such as the severe frontality – and stimuli from the Near East – for example the form of the beard – were integrated into the characteristic Cypriot style of the late sixth century BC.

HEAD OF ARISTOTLE
Roman copy after a Greek original
of c. 320 BC
Marble, height 29 cm
Inv. No. ANSA I 246

Images with portrait-like features can
occasionally be found in Greek art as
early as the fifth and fourth centuries
BC. Thus we encounter in the head of
Aristotle not the standard form of the
philosopher portrait, but a likeness with
pronounced individuality. The characteristic furrows of the 'thinker's brow' and
the small eyes lined with creases convey
the philosopher's advancing age. Aristotle was for a time the tutor of Alexander
the Great and founded a school of phi-
losophy in Athens, where a bronze statue with his facial features was erected.
The Vienna head, a Roman copy from
the first century AD, may be derived
from this model.

SARCOPHAGUS WITH FIGHTING AMAZONS
Greek: Late Classical, c. 320 BC
From Soloi (Cyprus)
Marble, height 91.4 cm, width 264.8 cm,
depth 104 cm
Inv. No. ANSA I 169

The relief art of Greek stone sarcophagi
reached its first apogee not in the
motherland, but among the Greeks in
the East. Thus it was that the sarcophagus was discovered in a burial
chamber in Cyprus in the sixteenth
century and found its way to Vienna
via the Fuggers, a notable family of
Augsburg merchants. The Greek heroes'
struggle against the mythical female
warriors is dramatically played out in
a series of individual, symmetrically
composed scenes. In the central group
a Greek attempts to save his fallen
comrade while defending himself with
his shield against the axe blows of an
Amazon.

ARTEMIS OF LARNACA

Hellenistic, late second century BC
from Kition (Larnaca, Cyprus)
Marble, height 78 cm
Inv. No. ANSA I 603

Dressed in a long robe and cloak, Artemis is leaning against an ancient votive statue. We can identify her as the goddess of hunting by means of the strap that goes over her shoulder, supporting at one time the quiver on her back. Her right hand, clutching a torch, was supposedly still there when the statue was found. The figure of a girl, on which the goddess is propping herself up with her left hand, may constitute a venerable statue of Artemis herself, as she is familiar to us from ancient votive gifts. The late Archaic costume of the statue offers a deliberate contrast to the rich folds of Artemis' garments. This Hellenistic masterpiece was found near the ancient city of Kition on the island of Cyprus.

HEAD OF JUPITER

Roman, first century AD
Bronze, hollow cast, height 29 cm
Inv. No. ANSA VI 9

The head comes from the Ambras
Castle collection of Archduke Ferdinand
of Tyrol and was originally part of a
statue. Today the eyes – which would
have been in coloured material and set
in – are missing, as is the thin copper
plating that once covered the lips.
Jupiter's face is framed by the hair and
beard in a carefully wrought wreath of
curls. The head is an outstanding example of the classicism of the early imperial period, which adopted the stylistic
features and tendencies of older epochs
of Greek art and recast them as its own,
Roman works.

GRIMANI RELIEF

Roman, first half of the first century AD
From Praeneste (Palestrina, Italy)
Marble, height 94 cm, width 81 cm
Inv. No. ANSA I 605

In a grotto at the foot of a gnarled
plane tree a lioness, looking around vigi-
lantly, suckles her twin cubs. Near the
tree is a small rustic shrine to the god
Dionysus consisting of a stone-built altar
with fruit, a votive relief adorned with
garlands as well as two of the god's
attributes: a torch and thyrsus rod
crowned with a pine cone. The compan-
ion piece to this idyllic relief, which is
also to be found in the Collection of
Greek and Roman Antiquities, shows a
suckling ewe. Both works found their
way to Vienna from the Palazzo Grimani
in Venice and belonged to a Roman
well in the ancient city of Praeneste to
the south-east of Rome. A third relief
also uncovered there shows a suckling
wild sow.

SARCOPHAGUS WITH LION HUNT

Roman, 270–290 AD
Marble, height 74 cm, width 212 cm
Inv. No. ANSA I 1133

The lively scene on this sarcophagus
depicts the deceased on horseback on
a wild animal hunt, surrounded by his
companions and servants. Battling a lion
with his lance, he is accompanied by
Virtus, an embodiment of his courage
and virtue as a huntsman. In antiquity
the lion hunt was a privilege of princes
and kings, so the choice of subject is an
indication of the high social rank of the
deceased. The iconography derives
from representations of animal fights
and lion hunts in the Roman circus.
The lion is also understood generally

as a tomb guardian and as a symbol of victory, and at either end of the sarcophagus the animal is shown with an antelope that it has savaged. The unfinished faces of the lord of the hunt and of Virtus indicate that sarcophagi such as this one were produced in advance.

MITHRAS RELIEF

Roman, second half of the second century AD
From Monastero near Aquileia (Italy)
Marble, height 61 cm
Inv. No. ANSA I 624

The relief shows the central scene in the cult of the Persian god of light Mithras: the killing of the bull in a cave. This act, several hundred representations of which are known from the Roman Empire, is symbolic of the regeneration of the world. Snake, scorpion and dog feed on the dying bull, from whose tail grows an ear of corn. The astronomical aspects of the cult are expressed by means of the sun in a quadriga on the left and the moon in a sickle on the right. Mithras' attendants, dressed like him in Persian costume, symbolise with their raised and lowered torches the winter and summer solstices.

This mystery cult was an ancient esoteric doctrine, about which very little is known today. In the second and third centuries AD it spread rapidly through the empire, in particular its western provinces.

GEOMETRIC PITCHER

Attic, second half of the eighth century BC
From Athens (Greece)
Clay, height 51 cm, diameter 27.7 cm
Inv. No. ANSA IV 2

The ninth and eighth centuries BC have come to be designated the 'Geometric Period' on account of the decoration of vases. In the pottery workshops of Athens, which developed this style and left their mark on it, vessels of often considerable size were produced for use as grave goods. Geometrical patterns, such as meanders, triangles and circles, are the characteristic motifs; the rare figurative representations (burial ceremonies, animals), which only appeared in the eighth century, are also characterised by geometrical features. This richly decorated pitcher with lid, the knob of which is in the form of a miniature cup, was created in the Late Geometric Period. The sketchy, 'impressionistic' style of painting is typical of this time.

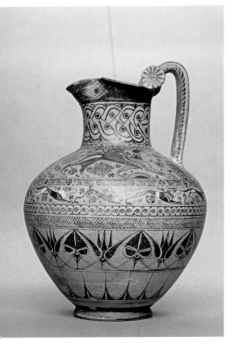

RHODIAN JUG

East Greek, c. 600 BC
From Siana (Rhodes)
Clay, height 38 cm, diameter 25.5 cm
Inv. No. ANSA IV 1622

Vase painting of the seventh century BC is characterised by strongly Orientalising influences, geometric ornamentation having now been superseded by new motifs from the plant and animal kingdoms. The leading role of Athens was taken over by Corinth, with further centres emerging in East Greece. This *Rhodian Jug,* named after the place where the majority of vessels of this kind were found, gives us a good insight into the development of this style in the Greek East: circular animal friezes (sphinxes and a griffin, dogs and hares) as well as ornamental bands with interlacing patterns and lotus blossoms cover the white surface of the vessel's body. The style of painting that combines closed silhouettes with outline drawings, the elongation of the figures and the wealth of ornamental decoration lends the jug a particular charm.

AMPHORA: DIONYSOS

Attic, black figure, Affected Painter,
C. 540 BC
Clay, height 44.9 cm, diameter 29 cm
Inv. No. ANSA IV 4399

Gods and heroes are among the favourite pictorial themes of Attic vase painting of the sixth century BC. The scene on this black-figure amphora – a storage jar for wine or oil – depicts the arrival of the wine god Dionysos in Athens: the bearded, ivy-crowned god looks dignified in amongst a group of men; he holds the kantharos – his ritual drinking vessel – in his right hand and a vine in his left. The Athenian Ikarios, who was taught the art of viticulture by Dionysos, raises his hand in salutation. The manneristic style of painting, whereby a more animated way of representing figures is sacrificed in favour

HYDRIA: BUSIRIS

East Greek, black figure, Busiris Painter,
C. 510 BC
From Caere (Cerveteri, Italy)
Clay, height 45 cm, diameter 37 cm
Inv. No. ANSA IV 3576

This three-handled water jar is part of a group of Caeretan hydriae that were produced in a workshop run by Ionian Greeks who had emigrated to Etruria. ('Caeretan' refers to the principal place where the jars were found, namely Caere). According to legend, the Egyptian king Busiris sacrificed all foreigners to Zeus. When Heracles came to Egypt, he let himself be led to the altar in shackles, then tore off his bonds and killed Busiris and his retinue. The main picture shows in colourful exuberance and naivety the punishment meted out to the king. The lower figure frieze depicts a hunting scene, possibly the Calydonian boar hunt.

of the overall decorative impression, earned the Attic potter his epithet 'Affected Painter'.

DOURIS CUP
Attic, red figure,
painted by Douris, *c.* 500 BC
From Caere (Cerveteri, Italy)
Clay, height 13 cm,
diameter 33 cm
Inv. No. ANSA IV 3694

The red-figure style of painting – a reversal of the process used in the black-figure style – was developed in Athens around 530 BC. The whole vessel was covered in black glaze except for the figures and decorative elements, which were left blank and thus appear in the original red colour of the clay. The drawing now took on a freer form, since the details (hair, beard, drapery folds) no longer had to be incised with a sharp instrument but could be applied using a fine paintbrush.

Douris, one of the most important Attic vase painters of the early fifth century, used the new technique to paint this magnificent drinking cup with scenes that give us a glimpse into the world of the warrior. The interior picture shows a scene of parting: a woman serves a farewell libation from a jug to a bearded, armed warrior who holds a bowl in his right hand.

SKYPHOS OF THE BRYGOS PAINTER
Attic, red figure, Brygos Painter, c. 490 BC
From Caere (Cerveteri, Italy)
Clay, height 25 cm, diameter 31.6 cm
Inv. No. ANSA IV 3710

Depicted on this large drinking bowl, which was made in the workshop of the potter Brygos, is a scene from Homer's *Iliad*. Achilles, the legendary hero of the Greeks in the Trojan War, reclines on a couch in front of which a small table is laid out with food. Priam, the aged King of Troy, approaches with his retinue from the left in order to beg for the body of his fallen son Hector, which is lying beneath the kline; to the right stands the cup-bearer of Achilles, with ladle and wine-sieve in his hands.

The ransom of Hector was already a well-known theme in Archaic pictorial art of the sixth century BC, but in no earlier representation is sympathy with the fate of the aged Trojan king so keenly aroused as in this scene. His delight in story-telling and his love of detail place the painter – named the Brygos Painter after the potter – among the most important vase painters of the early fifth century BC.

CENTAUR
Hellenistic (Seleucid), c. 160 BC
From Falerii (Civita Castellana, Italy)
Silver, partly gilded, height 22 cm
Inv. No. ANSA VIIa 49

What is depicted here is not one of those unbridled hybrid creatures with a horse's body, whose struggle against the Lapiths had symbolic meaning for the Greeks, but rather a music-making centaur such as Chiron, the tutor of the young Achilles. His left hand would once have held a stringed instrument, while his right hand still holds a plectrum. With its strong pathos and the rich modelling of the body, the figure is closely related stylistically to the relief of the great frieze of the *Pergamon Altar* (Pergamon Museum, Berlin). From a technical point of view as well, the centaur, which was probably part of a rhyton (a drinking horn), can be counted among the masterpieces of ancient toreutics (metalwork). Except for the arms and legs, which are cast, the entire body is chased from a single piece of silver sheet.

SENATUS CONSULTUM DE BACCHANALIBUS
See page 56
Roman: Republican, 186 BC
From Tiriolo (Calabria, Italy)
Bronze, height 27.3 cm, width 28.5 cm
(without frame)
Inv. No. ANSA III 168

This famous bronze tablet carries the oldest surviving senatorial decree in the Latin language. It sets out the prohibition of the Bacchanalia (rites for the god Dionysos/Bacchus). Festivals in honour of the god resulted in ecstatic riots, with adherents of

the cult moreover coming under suspicion of plotting to jeopardise the state.

The present, sole surviving copy of the edict was intended for a rural community in southern Italy, namely Ager Teuranus (modern-day Tiriolo in Calabria). It also includes the instruction that the stipulations and the penalties for offences be announced in a public meeting and that they be displayed publicly. The tablet was found in the year 1640 and set in a Baroque tortoiseshell frame.

EMPEROR AUGUSTUS
(REIGNED 27 BC–14 AD)
Roman: Augustan, early first century AD
Marble, height 36 cm
Inv. No. ANSA I 60

This monumental head corresponds very precisely with the prototype of the Augustan portrait, the creation of which is connected with the bestowal of the honorary name Augustus ('the noble one') and the changed status of the ruler from 27 BC onwards.

The head is slightly turned to the right, the strained forehead with two short steep folds over the bridge of the nose lending the portrait a concentrated expression. The facial features are serene and only broken up by small irregularities. The characteristic hairstyle of the portrait of Augustus is identifiable in the curl motif of the forelock ('fork' and 'pincers').

The moulding of the figure harks back to the high Classical sculpture of the Greek sculptor Polyclitos, the classicist style expressing the changed self-image of the subject.

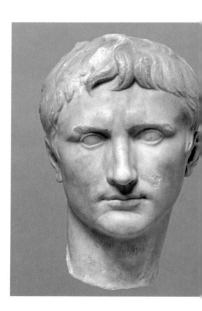

PORTRAIT OF A YOUNG ROMAN

Roman: Early Hadrianic, 120–130 AD
Marble, height 34 cm
Inv. No. ANSA I 1768

In this very high-quality portrait the individual features of the subject are shown to particularly good advantage. The head, originally part of a bust, turns energetically to the left, the facial expression however remaining serene and concentrated. The well-ordered forelocks and the short sideburns emphasize the smart appearance of the beardless young man.

The type, the style of sculpture and the hairstyle indicate that the portrait was produced before or around the year 120 AD. It shows a variant of the courtly portrait which was very popular under Hadrian, and which anticipated the subsequent imperial portraits (for example those of Marcus Aurelius).

MUMMY PORTRAIT: WOMAN WITH NECKLACE

Roman: Middle to Late Antonine, 161–192 AD
From er-Rubayat (Egypt)
Encaustic on wood, height 36.5 cm, width 21.5 cm, depth 0.9 cm
Inv. No. ANSA X 301

With the conquest of Egypt by Emperor Augustus the custom grew up of binding a painted portrait to the face of the mummy. This practice is closely connected with the ancient Egyptian desire to preserve the facial features of the deceased for the afterlife.

The lifelike portrait of a smiling woman – painted in hot wax (encaustic) on wood – comes, like most of the surviving mummy portraits, from the Fayum oasis. The lady is wearing a reddish-pink garment with ornamental braid trimming, gold drop earrings with pearls and two golden necklaces. One of them has a Medusa's head as a pendant. The simple pinned-up hair and the facial features of the young woman with the large eyes are modelled on portraits of the young Faustina, the wife of the Roman emperor Marcus Aurelius.

EMPRESS ARIADNE
Late Antiquity/Early Byzantine,
C. 500 AD
Ivory, height 26.5 cm, width 12.7 cm,
max. depth 1.9 cm
Inv. No. ANSA X 39

In late antiquity a multipartite decorative art form developed out of the customary two-part writing tablet, the so-called diptych. This precious ivory panel with the image of an empress, once gilded, is the central section of what would have been a five-part polyptych. It conveys a striking picture of Byzantine court ceremonial, which differs markedly from that depicted on monuments of the preceding Roman imperial period. Dressed in richly ornamented regalia, the ruler is enthroned beneath a baldachin. In her left hand she holds the globe surmounted by the cross. Individual traits are almost completely suppressed in favour of the conventional representation of the sovereign's power. This complicates the identification of the empress, but she is probably Ariadne (died 515 AD), wife of the Byzantine emperors Zenon and Anastasius.

PORTRAIT OF EUTROPIOS

Late Roman: late Theodosian,
middle of the fifth century AD
From Ephesos (Turkey)
Marble, height 32 cm
Inv. No. ANSA I 880

This expressive bust of an old man is generally identified with Eutropios, a citizen of Ephesos who, in a Greek inscription on a console found nearby, is described as the donor of the paving of the streets of the city. The head is facing forwards, the almost impassive face elongated. The eyes are wide open and made all the more prominent by the fixed gaze and the long-distance stare. The short, slightly wavy hair billows over the temples in cap-like fashion and leaves the ears uncovered. The portrait was created in a style characteristic of late antiquity – formally abstract and transcending individual traits – and corresponds with the portrait type of a high-ranking official of a Roman provincial metropolis. The abstraction of the subject's outward appearance reflects the development of Roman society towards the strictly hierarchical Byzantine state dominated by court ceremonial.

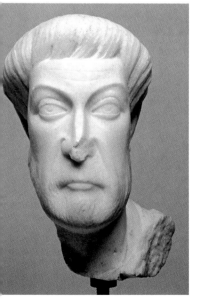

PTOLEMAIC CAMEO

See page 60, above
Hellenistic, 278–270/69 BC
Eleven-layered onyx; setting:
gold surround; sixteenth century (?),
height 11.5 cm, width 11.3 cm
Inv. No. ANSA IXa 81

The magnificent cameos of antiquity are miniature works of art of the highest artistic quality. Their fascination lies as much in their subject matter – providing insights into the politics, cultural history and religion of their age – as in their technical virtuosity and the precious materials from which they are made. Cameos were used for purposes of political representation as well as serving the glorification of the ruler and his family; they were highlights of the imperial treasuries. While intaglios are deeply incised (they were often used as seals), cameos are embossed miniature reliefs, in other words carved out of the stone, so that for the most part the figures are worked in the light layer, the background being formed by the dark layer. The portraits of an Egyptian royal couple are cut out of the stone's eleven layers, alternately dark brown and bluish white. Ptolemy II Philadelphos in the foreground wears an Attic helmet with cheek-pieces depicting a thunderbolt, the attribute of Zeus. The serpent on the crest of the helmet is the Hellenized descendant of the uraeus snake on the war helmet of the Egyptian pharaohs. On the neck-piece of the helmet can be seen the head of the Egyptian god Ammon. In the background Ptolemy's sister and wife Arsinoë II wears a bonnet-like crown under a veil. The cameo was fashioned some time between the pair's nuptials in 278 BC and the death of Arsinoë in 270/69. It may have served as an official wedding present. According to the description given by the theologian and natural scientist Albertus Magnus, the cameo was to be seen in the *Shrine of the Three Kings* in Cologne around the middle of the

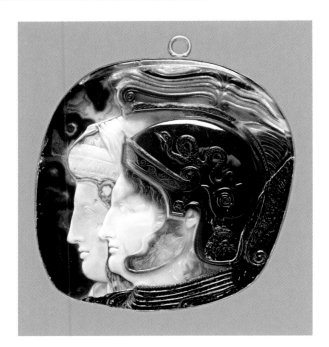

thirteenth century. At that time, the
heads of the ruling couple and of
Ammon were interpreted as an image
of the three Magi from the East. In 1574
the precious stone was stolen. The
cameo turned up again in Rome in 1586
and was acquired by Vincenzo Gonzaga
for his collection in Mantua. It was first
recorded in Vienna in the year 1668/9.

EAGLE CAMEO
Roman, 27 BC
Two-layered onyx; setting: silver gilt,
Milan, third quarter of the sixteenth century;
diameter 22 cm
Inv. No. ANSA IXa 26

The eagle, symbol of the might of the
Roman Empire, stands with outstretched
wings on a palm branch. In its left, raised

talon it is carrying a wreath of oak leaves. The image refers to the honours that were conferred on Octavian on 16 January 27 BC in gratitude for his having saved Rome from the chaos of civil war; these honours included bestowing on him the name 'Augustus' and attaching an oak wreath, the *corona civica* (civic crown), over the door of his house. The State cameos were in the possession of the imperial treasury in Rome, from where they probably found their way to Byzantium in the fifth century AD. In 1204 the crusaders brought them back to the West after the sacking of Constantinople. Immediately afterwards the *Eagle Cameo* was probably affixed to the ambo of King Henry II in the cathedral at Aachen. It was first recorded in Vienna in 1750.

GEMMA AUGUSTEA

Roman, 9–12 AD
Double-layered sardonyx; setting: gold frame reverse in ornamented openwork, German, seventeenth century,
height 19 cm, width 23 cm
Inv. No. ANSA IXa 79

The most important ancient cameo preserved today in the Vienna Collection of Greek and Roman Antiquities – the *Gemma Augustea* – served to glorify the deeds of Emperor Augustus and his successor Tiberius. It is cut from a double-layered Arabian sardonyx stone and is a masterpiece of the imperial gem workshop in Rome.

In the upper register Augustus is enthroned in the apparel and pose of Jupiter, in his hands the sceptre and augur's staff. To the right of the emperor sits Roma, the protectress of the city. Between the heads of the two figures is the Capricorn (Augustus' sign of the zodiac), at his feet the eagle. On the right-hand side is a group of allegorical figures: Oecumene, the inhabited world,

Oceanus, the personification of the sea, as well as Italia with her cornucopia and two boys. Next to Rome stands Germanicus, great-nephew of Augustus, dressed as an officer. On the left-hand side Tiberius, the crown prince and step-son of the emperor, is stepping out of a biga that is being driven by Victoria. In the lower register gods are erecting a tropaion (a victory monument) and introducing captive Barbarians. The scene may refer to the defeat of the Dalmatian insurrection: on 16 January AD 10 Tiberius, the supreme comman-der-in-chief of the Roman troops, entered Rome, where he appeared before the emperor as victor.

The cameo is first documented in 1246 in an inventory of Saint-Sernin Abbey in Toulouse. At the beginning of the seventeenth century it found its way into Habsburg hands when it was pur-chased by Rudolf II.

HEROPHILOS GLASS CAMEO
Roman, c. 20 AD
Glass; modern setting: gold surround,
height 5.9 cm
Inv. No. ANSA IXa 30

This cameo with the portrait head of a man wearing a laurel wreath still preserves the signature of Herophilos (to the right of his neck: 'ΗΡΟΦΙΛΟC ΔΙΟCΚΟΥΡΙΔ[ΟΥ]' 'Herophilos, son of Dioscurides'), who was active under Emperor Tiberius (AD 14–37) as im-perial gem cutter. The cameo is not a cut stone, but an antique glass copy cast after the original by Herophilos, which mimics a turquoise in its blue colour tinged with green. The portrait probably represents Drusus the Elder or his son Germanicus and constitutes a posthumous honorary portrait which Emperor Tiberius commissioned in memory of his brother or his nephew. Glass casts of the original masterpiece, whose value was raised by the inclu-sion of a gold coating, achieved wide

circulation as imperial gifts or were awarded as medals for military service.

GEMMA CLAUDIA
Roman, c. 49 AD
Five-layered onyx; setting: gold surround,
height 12 cm
Inv. No. ANSA IXa 63

Out of two double cornucopias sprout two pairs of portrait busts ranged one behind the other: on the left is Emperor Claudius (reigned 41–54 AD) and his fourth wife Agrippina the Younger (15/16–59 AD); opposite them are the parents of the bride – Germanicus (15 BC–19 AD), the brother of the emperor, and Agrippina the Elder (14 BC–33 AD). The cameo was prob-ably created on the occasion of the wedding of the emperor. The cornu-copias symbolise the expectation of abundant blessings, while the eagle and weapons refer to the victorious Emperor.

An unknown master carved the scene with great skill from five alternately dark and light layers. He achieves an increased transparency of the material by cutting exquisitely thin layers in places (min. thickness of the base 2 mm).

APOLLO

Roman: Early Augustan,
second half of the first century BC
From Transsylvania (Romania)
Bronze, hollow cast, height 28.5 cm
Inv. No. ANSA VI 2848

Apollon (Roman name Apollo) is the Greek god of crops and oracles, the god of the Muses and of light and the averter of evil. The naked god once held in his lowered right hand a bough and in his left the laurel stem, the symbol of purifying, atoning power. In the statuette, older stylistic features are mixed with newer ones, the hairstyle with the long spiralling locks contrasting with the powerful, modelled body. Apart from achieving a decorative charm, the return to older stylistic elements was probably also intended to convey the great antiquity of the cult of Apollo. The statuette, which is known as the *Apollo of Transsylvania* after the place where it was found, once belonged to a Roman domestic shrine (lararium).

BUST OF JUPITER
Roman, after a Greek model from the
second half of the fourth century BC
Bronze, height 17.5 cm
Inv. No. ANSA VI 288

The bust, which was already documented in Rome before 1700, was part of a
set. In his hair Jupiter (Greek name Zeus)
wears an oak wreath. A cloth is laid
across the back of his head; it falls over
the left side of his body and onto his
right shoulder. The covering of the head
is of sacred significance. His hair rises
high over his wrinkled brow in the manner of the portraits of Alexander the
Great and frames his large face with
wavy, softly modelled curls. A winged
thunderbolt, the weapon of Jupiter, leans
against the right side of the bust.

**YOUTH FROM
THE MAGDALENSBERG**
Sixteenth-century cast copy after a
Roman original
From the Magdalensberg (Carinthia, Austria)
Bronze, height 185 cm
Inv. No. ANSA VI 1

In 1983 the Collection of Greek and
Roman Antiquities launched a research
project which was primarily intended to
clarify the techniques used in casting
and moulding the Magdalensberg *Youth*.
The results were surprising: the statue is
not the antique original, but rather a
cast copy dating from the sixteenth century. The original was found in 1502 by
a farmer while he was ploughing.
Through Matthäus Lang von Wellenburg,
initially Bishop of Gurk and then from
1519 Archbishop of Salzburg, the statue
found its way to Salzburg. The news of
this sensational find spread quickly: thus
Albrecht Dürer may perhaps have seen
the *Youth* in 1505 during a trip he made
to Italy. As early as 1534 it was published
as a woodcut in a book of epigraphs, and
in 1542 there followed a fresco by the
Salzburg painter Hans Bocksberger the
Elder at the palace of the Dukes of
Bavaria in Landshut. In 1551 the Salzburg
Cathedral chapter complied with a
request from Ferdinand I and presented
the *Youth* to the king. (The minutes
concerning this instruction still exist.)
So that they might retain at least a copy,
the canons had a cast made. With the
passage of time knowledge of this
occurrence was lost, so that the cast was
taken to be the original, and as such
entered the Vienna collection of classical
antiquities in 1806. The original has disappeared, but it might have reached
Spain in the second half of the sixteenth
century.

The most significant indication that the
statue is a Renaissance copy and not the
antique original lies in the technique of
its moulding and casting: the *Youth* was
made with the help of negatives taken
from the original, and cast in a technique
that was unknown in antiquity but which
was in use in the sixteenth century.
Associated with this technique are the
thickness of the bronze and the fact
that it was cast in one piece. Scientific
investigations (radiography, analysis of
the alloy and the core of the cast etc)
yielded further important evidence. The
clear signs of reworking on the surface
(hammer, file and scraper marks) are

partly attributable, as already suggested earlier, to a later revision, but in the main derive from cold work undertaken at the rough casting stage. A complete glazing of the surface was dispensed with; the statue was given a black lacquer-like coating, of which a few traces still remain.

We do not know either the exact year of production (after 1551) or the workshop in which the casting took place, but the statue in Vienna is in any case one of the earliest Renaissance cast copies of a large-scale antique bronze. The original is regarded as a work of Roman ideal sculpture from the first century BC, modelled on Classical Greek sculptures (Polyclitus). According to the inscription on the right thigh, which we must assume was also on the original, the creation of the Magdalensberg statue was funded by two freedmen, Aulus Poblicius Antiocus and Tiberius Barbius Tiberi(a)nus.

GRIFFIN

Roman: Early Imperial, first half of the first century AD
From the Magdalensberg (Carinthia, Austria)
Bronze, height 40 cm
Inv. No. ANSA VI 324

The composite creature from the Orient consisting of a winged lion's body and an eagle's head already existed as a motif in Creto-Mycenean art. The superbly executed statuette was found on the Magdalensberg in Carinthia and belonged to a group with Apollo, who propped his stringed instrument up against the distinctive bridge between the two erect wings of the animal. Sitting with raised right forepaw, the griffin gazes up towards the god with rapt attention and waits for him to start playing again. The statuette is certainly not the product of a local workshop, but must have been imported from Italy.

STATUETTE OF JUPITER DOLICHENUS

Roman, first half of the third century AD
From Mauer an der Url (near Amstetten
in Lower Austria)
Bronze, height (with pedestal) 32 cm
Inv. No. ANSA M 1

With more than 100 objects, this Roman
find is one of the most extensive ever
made on Austrian soil. Uncovered in the
vicinity of the Roman fort of Mauer an
der Url (near Amstetten, Lower Austria),
together they make up the mobile
inventory of a shrine to the god Jupiter
Dolichenus. His cult was transplanted
to the West from the Syrian city of
Doliche chiefly by soldiers, whose
patron he was. The hoard, which was
buried in the first half of the third
century AD through fear of one of the
many Germanic incursions, gives an
impression of the inventory of a provincial shrine on the periphery of the

Roman Empire (the province of
Noricum). The objects pertain both
to the religious sphere (statuettes,
standards, silver votive plates) and to
the secular (vessels, lamps, bells, implements and tools).
Jupiter Dolichenus stands on the back
of a bull, dressed in Phrygian cap,
cuirass and half-boots, in his hands the
thunderbolt and double axe (of which
only the handle remains). The god on
the bull appears again within the hoard;
he forms a group with his consort,
Juno, who is represented standing on
a hind.

FIBULA

Roman: Late Antique, second third of
the fifth century AD
From Nagymihály (Michalovce, Slovakia)
Gold, inlays: onyx, garnet, amethyst, glass
paste, length 19.5 cm, weight 160.1 g
Inv. No. ANSA VIIb 307

A network of variously cut garnets (cloi-
sonné technique) frames the precious,
two-layered onyx in the centre of this
gilded fibula. Further decorative elements include glass inlays, semi-circular
garnets and amethysts in single settings
as well as little gold spheres that have
been stuck on. The border is decorated
with a spiral pattern forming cells filled
with glass paste. This splendid cloak pin
was found in 1852 in the formerly Hungarian town of Rebrény near Nagymihály
(modern-day Michalovce, East Slovakia).
With its three pendant chains set with
precious stones it recalls the sumptuous
disc-shaped fibulae worn by emperors in
late antiquity and during the Byzantine
period.

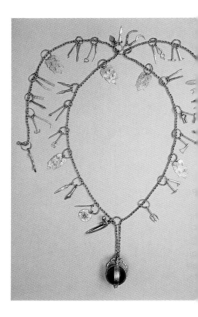

GOLD CHAIN WITH FIFTY-TWO PENDANTS

Germanic, c. 400 AD
From Szilágysomlyó (Şimleu Silvaniei,
Romania)
Gold (22.3 carat), smoky quartz,
length (without globe pendant) 176 cm
Inv. No. ANSA VIIb 1

In 1797 two shepherd boys in Szilágysomlyó (present-day Şimleu Silvaniei,
Romania) stumbled by chance across a
hoard of gold. It comprised a series of
originally seventeen gold medallions,
one garnet-encrusted pendant, metal
rings and additional items of gold jewellery as well as a unique gold necklace
with a total of fifty-two amulet-like
pendants. The focal point of this necklace is a smoky quartz sphere in a
cruciate setting, with two lions standing
on either side of a mixing vessel.
The other pendants show a man in a
dug-out boat, tools, implements and
weapons in miniature form as well as
small vine leaves. The chain served as
body jewellery for a woman and was
worn over the breast and back.

Almost a hundred years later (1889) a further treasure trove was recovered on the same plot of land. Today it is in the Magyar Nemzeti Múzeum in Budapest. Both finds are indeed part of a single hoard, which was collected by an East Germanic family of the highest rank over several generations and buried around the second quarter of the fifth century AD in two different locations.

PAIR OF FIBULAE

East Germanic, beginning of the fifth century AD
From Untersiebenbrunn (Lower Austria)
Gold plate over silver, stone inlays, glass, enamel, length respectively 15.9 and 16 cm
Inv. Nos. ANSA U 1 and U 2

These two precious ornamental fibulae were found among the grave contents of the so-called 'Princess of Untersieben-brunn' – indisputably the most important find on Austrian soil from the time of the Great Migration. The exceptionally richly furnished tomb containing the skeleton of a twenty- to twenty-four-year old woman was discovered by accident in 1910. It contained valuable jewellery, clothing elements and toilet articles of precious metal, glass drinking vessels and sections of a bridle for a saddle-horse and harness for two draught horses. The two magnificent bow fibulae are made of cast silver. The surface of both is covered with gold plate and is decorated with different coloured inlays set in cells (some raised, some flat-cut semi-precious stones, predominantly garnets, but also glass and enamel). Gold wires and granulation balls make up further decorative elements.

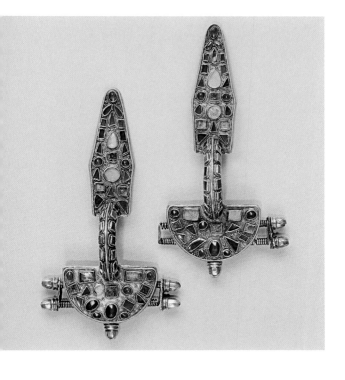

HOARD OF GOLD
FROM NAGYSZENTMIKLÓS

Early Middle Ages, seventh to ninth
century AD
From Nagyszentmiklós
(Sânnicolau Mare, Romania)
Gold, total weight 9,926 g
Medallion jug: first half of the eighth
century AD (?)
Gold (18 carat), height 22 cm
Inv. No. ANSA VIIb 33

The largest yet known early medieval gold hoard came to light in 1799 near the formerly Hungarian town of Nagyszentmiklós (present-day Sânnicolau Mare, Romania). It comprises twenty-three gold vessels with a total weight of nearly 10 kg. On first inspection the jugs, bowls, cups, goblets and drinking horn present a uniform character, but in fact they were produced at different times and some have been reworked. Thus, for example, the jugs were originally conceived as flasks and were only subsequently fitted with handles. Avarian elements coexist alongside Sassanid and Roman-Byzantine, mythical creatures next to the Christian cross. Many vessels bear inscriptions partly in Greek lettering or rather (more often) in a runiform script, which has not be satisfactorily interpreted to date. On account of the heterogeneity and the uniqueness of the treasure trove very diverse attributions and datings have been proposed. The most recent research accepts a connection with the Avars.

On the jug with medallions four circular arrays framed by ornamental bands show figurative scenes: an eagle is carrying off a woman, and a rider astride a fabulous creature is aiming at a panther. A group of animals fighting can also be seen (a griffin is attacking a fallow deer). The most famous shows a knight on horseback, who is dragging a prisoner by the hair; from the saddle hangs the decapitated head of an enemy.

Kunstkammer

III. on pages 72/73:
Julius Victor Berger, "The Patrons of the
Visual Arts in the House of Habsburg",
ceiling painting in Hall XIX, detail.

The Kunstkammer (Collection of Sculpture and Decorative Arts) at the *Kunst-historisches Museum* evolved from the Habsburg treasuries (Schatzkammern) and art cabinets (Kunstkammern) of the late Middle Ages and the Renaissance and Baroque periods. Individual members of the dynasty who were enthusiastic collectors, and who mostly acted as patrons as well, added considerably to the holdings. The following collections are the basis of the present-day Kunstkammer:

• The Wunderkammer (curiosities cabinet) of Ferdinand II of Tyrol (1529–1595), which was first set up at Ambras Castle near Innsbruck. It contained most of the surviving items from older collections of the Emperors Frederick III, Maximilian I and Ferdinand I;

• The Kunstkammer (art cabinet) of Emperor Rudolf II (1552–1612), which originated in Prague. Many of Rudolf's treasures were permanently lost to the successor collection when Prague Castle was looted during the Thirty Years' War, but items previously brought to Vienna compensated for the losses with outstanding items of gold and stone-carving dating from the period around 1600, as well as masterly bronzes;

• In the seventeenth century, the items of the Kunstkammer of Archduke Leopold Wilhelm (1614–1662), brother of Emperor Ferdinand III and governor of the Netherlands, were added. Although he is famous mainly as one of the founders of the picture collection, Archduke Leopold bought not only large numbers of Italian paintings but also superb Renaissance bronzes, and collected small sculptures of stone, ivory and wood;

• Finally there was the Viennese Treasury (Schatzkammer), originally the oldest Habsburg collection, which in the seventeenth century gained not only works of semi-precious stones – always popular at the Viennese court – but also items of turned ivory, carvings of rhinoceros horn and miniature wax models.

In order to protect it from Napoleon's troops, the collection from Ambras Castle was moved to Vienna, where it was temporarily housed as a separate entity in the Lower Belvedere palace. From 1875, as part of the reorganisation of the imperial collections during the reign of Franz Joseph I, all the Kunstkammer collections were brought together under the roof of the new *Kunsthistorisches Museum,* opened in 1891. Only items of an insignia nature and those relating to members of the imperial dynasty were left in the Treasury.

The new collection was accommodated on the upper ground floor of the building, where it was first described as a "Sammlung kunstindustrieller Gegenstände" ("Collection of Art Industry Objects"), then renamed equally inappropriately in 1919 as the "Sculpture and Arts & Crafts Collection". However, as it only contained a small number of large sculptures and virtually no functional arts and crafts objects, in 1990 it was decided to go back to the original term *Kunstkammer* (art cabinet). The objects preserved here are predominantly non-functional. The most important parts of the collection, with their large numbers of items of gold work and stone-carving, bronze statuettes and figures and turned pieces made of ivory, often owe their very existence to the fastidious demands of a princely collector.

An art cabinet of this kind was to some extent a mirror of the cosmos and the sum of human knowledge about the world at that time. That is why it contained not only works of art *(artefacts)* but also remarkable products of nature and exotica; scientific instruments (the equipment required to investigate the cosmos); the printed graphics that documented all this; and finally curiosities (the so-called *mirabilia* or "wonders" of nature, science and craft) and works of art. *Kunstkammer* pieces were thus non-utilitarian showpieces of the highest material,

Julius Victor Berger, "The Patrons of the Visual Arts in the House of Habsburg", ceiling painting in Hall XIX, detail.

artistic and technical quality, rarities from nature and scientific instruments, which often represented pioneer achievements in technical development. In this way, art cabinets became a microcosm reflecting the world over which the prince had sway. As in this case the emperor or a member of the imperial dynasty was involved, the *Kunstkammer* was expected not only to be universal but also to contain objects of the highest quality. That is why even today the Vienna *Kunstkammer* has no serious rival and is at the same time as regards inventory one of the best-documented art collections in the world.

The high quality of the collections was legendary even in the sixteenth and seventeenth centuries. Quite a number of European princes considered it an honour to enhance the collection by presenting suitable items as gifts. It is known, for example, that Emperor Rudolf II was particularly receptive to 'diplomatic' offerings of this kind. From the eighteenth century the artistic ambitions of the Habsburgs turned more and more towards architecture, music and the theatre. They later devoted their time and attention to the reorganisation of the collections and the construction of the Kunsthistorisches Museum, whilst continuing to augment the collection by important individual additions.

After the collapse of the monarchy in 1918, the collections of the extinct Este family (Duchy of Modena) were added. In 1921, the collection of tapestries hitherto administered by the *Gardemeuble* (Imperial Furniture Depository) was incorporated into the *Kunstkammer*. The latter constituted almost 800 tapestries that had originally formed part of the furnishings of the imperial castles and palaces. It is one of the most important collections of its kind, surpassed only by that of the Spanish crown. Shortly before the temporary extinction of Austria's sovereignty in 1938, the legacy of Gustav von Benda brought some exquisite masterpieces of the Early Florentine Renaissance to the Sculpture and Crafts Collection. The latter fortunately survived World War II with very few losses. Sad to say, it was the tapestry collection which suffered: the museum was forced to lend pieces to Berlin and Goering's holiday home Carinhall for display purposes, where they disappeared.

Since 1963, the whole collection has been re-united in the Kunsthistorisches Museum. In 2002, building and technical work required the *Kunstkammer* to be temporarily closed. The complete renovation and expansion of the premises plus the reorganisation and updating of the exhibition are intended to highlight the immense importance of this valuable collection.

ST. GREGORY WITH SCRIBES

Carolingian, 9th century
Ivory, height 20.5 cm,
width 12.5 cm
Inv. No. KK 8399

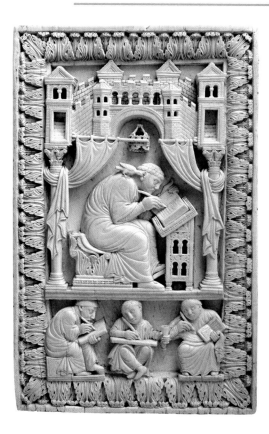

Pope Gregory the Great is considered to be the author of the Roman mass, the use of which Charlemagne made compulsory throughout the Carolingian empire. The sacramentary comprised the prayers spoken by the priest during the celebration of mass. In the Canon Missae, the core of the sacramentary, the preamble begins with the *Vere dignum*, the text that the divinely inspired Father of the Church has just formulated in the picture. His scribe had covertly noticed how the saint only resumed dictating when the dove of the Holy Ghost whispering in his ear fell silent. The moment of divine inspiration in this legend is what the scene records, though St. Gregory is now writing himself. The scribe crouching on the right in the lower part of the picture seems to be listening to the saint, but he is writing a different part of the text, as can be read with a magnifying glass. The copyists were thus duplicating the text of the Roman mass.

A Carolingian feature of this composition is the reduction of the external palatial architecture, which is to be interpreted as a long view. The dominant feature, the bridge-like central arch, is continued both in the flattened shape of the structure – a conglomeration of stairwells, walls, towers and arcaded galleries – and the curtain, though without an overall arch spanning the interior. The architecture indicates the spatial context as an interior, but also acts as an architectural frame for the picture of St. Gregory.

In this Frankish prototype, we may discern a predecessor of the architectural framings that developed in an artistic

dialogue on either side of the English Channel over 200 years and led to the beginning of the Romanesque style with the framing arch and the crown of a canopy as an exciting design idea. The structural composition of the overall picture is also Carolingian. Along with the baldachin frame, a great amount of other realistic detail is also taken over from an Early Byzantine model. However, contrary to the source, the scene, which broadens in the lower zone, is framed by a double-layered acanthus frieze that stops the whole compacted composition falling apart.

OLIPHANT
Southern Italian (Saracen), 11th century or first half of the 12th century
Ivory, partly coloured, length 51.8 cm
Inv. No. KK 4073

In the Middle Ages, "Saracen horns" were widely used as signals during hunting. This one is decorated on the body and mouthpiece with ornamental bands, while on the "bell" there is a broad figured frieze with hunting scenes and animals fighting. On the unadorned chamfered centre area of the oliphant is an inscription in a high-mediaeval script, probably added on

the occasion of its redesignation. It states that Count Albert III of Habsburg, grandfather of King Rudolf I, had given the horn filled with relics to the monastery of Muri in Switzerland as a gift. The transformation of valuable secular possessions into reliquaries was a frequent occurrence. In 1702, the oliphant returned to Habsburg ownership when the abbot of the time gave it to Emperor Leopold I.

GRIFFIN-SHAPED EWER (ACQUAMANILE)
Circle of Roger von Helmarshausen, first third of the 12th century
Gilt bronze, partially silver-encrusted, with niello, height 17.3 cm, length 14.5 cm, width 8.5 cm
Inv. No. KK 83

This ewer (acquamanile) radiates exotic charm. Its function as a utensil is transformed and fused in a symbiotic relationship with the demonic animal shape – an alertly erect bird with an eagle's beak, a griffin. Griffins were symbols of Christ as the purifier of the soul. Oriental-style ewers were often used for secular purposes: as noble, knightly utensils, they bear witness to the aristocratic culture of the time. Also well-documented is their use for washing the priest's hands during the liturgy. For example, in the treasury of Mainz Cathedral in 1253 were noted "pouring vessels of various shapes called *manilia*, because water is poured from them over the hands of the priests. Some of them had the shape of lions, others were dragons, griffins …]" etc.

The Viennese piece is associated with the circle of Roger von Helmarshausen, a monk who was active around 1100 in Lower Saxony and who was one of the greatest mediaeval artists in the field of church plate. The accomplished hollow casting in bronze looks perfect in the swelling roundness of its smooth shape and its elegant flowing lines. Flat applied decorative elements of damascene silver inlays and fused niello combined with overall fire gilding dominate the colouring, which is made up of the

black of the inlaid beads representing the eyes, anthracite grey, the gleam of silver and glow of gold. Though the artistic antecedents have hitherto been considered to be Mosan work, technical details of this kind are more typical of the Anglo-Saxon tradition. At the same time as Roger von Helmarshausen was active in Lower Saxony, the Gloucester Candlestick was produced in around 1107/13 in England, where the use of such inserted pupils made of silver inlays and niello decoration was common. Lower Saxon art, too, overcame the restrictions which otherwise drew a clear line between bronze casts and gold work.

FIRE-BLOWER (AEOLIPILE)
Northern Italian [?], first half of the
12th century
Bronze, height 23.5 cm
Inv. No. KK 5702

Whether this grotesque aeolipile (literally, 'ball of Aeolus') was simply a household item used like bellows for the fire or featured in experiments with steam power is not known. Filled with water and placed in the glowing embers, it puffed steam through small holes in the mouth and nose (the hole in the abdomen is the result of damage). Like this piece, antique versions kneeled or squatted and put a hand protectively to their foreheads. All mediaeval aeolopiles are naked and mostly depicted with prominent sexual parts. Perhaps this unusual item goes back far beyond the classical antecedents to prehistoric fertility symbols.

**COMMUNION CHALICE
(WILTEN CHALICE)**
Lower Saxony, c. 1160/70
Silver, part gilt, niello, height 16.7 cm
Inv. No. KK 8924

The celebration of mass required purpose-made altar utensils. Chalices and patens were ritually the most important because they came into contact with the holy sacrament. In Catholic doctrine, the bread and wine are changed by the words of the Communion into the body and blood of Christ in the

ands of the priest. The two Romanesque Communion chalices on display re two-handled Eucharistic chalices. hey were only used when the host was lso offered up with consecrated wine vhich the congregation drank through traws.

he series of images of the Salvation, omprising scenes from the Old and New Testaments and inscriptions on the halice and paten from Wilten Abbey, lustrate the meaning and importance f the Eucharistic offering. They culmiate on the paten in Christ's sacrifice on he Cross and his victory over death. On the base of the chalice there are cenes from the Old Testament, including the Fall of Man as the ultimate reaon for Christ's redeeming sacrifice as vell as the sacrifices of Noah, Abraham nd Melchisedek. On the outer sides of he cup there are New Testament scenes rom the Annunciation to the Carrying f the Cross. The events of the Last upper occupy a large area. Above the our cardinal virtues on the stem are the our rivers of paradise in relief on the

node. Their presence indicates that the chalice is a real fount of life bringing forth the blood of Christ. Probably at the prompting of Count Berthold III of Andechs (1148–1188) – if he is indeed the "BERTHOLDUS" mentioned as donor in the inscription – the altar plate was donated to Wilten Abbey. This superb example of the Romanesque goldsmiths' art is largely executed in niello for the sake of graphic effectiveness, and came from the circle of artists under the patronage of Henry the Lion.

COMMUNION CHALICE FROM ST. PETER'S ABBEY IN SALZBURG
Salzburg, c. 1160/80
Gilt silver, node of beryl, set with precious stones, height 23 cm
Inv. No. KK 9983

The inscription on the concealed edge of the base of the chalice indicates that the half-length figures growing from the pinnacles of the battlements are representatives of the Twelve Tribes of Israel under the leadership of Aaron.

The budding of Aaron's rod meant that God had appointed the Levites to be the priestly caste. There is a direct link from the high priests of the Old Testament to Christ. The inscription around the rim of the chalice relates to the Twelve Representatives of the Old Testament after Moses, who pray for the blood of Christ to redeem what has been destroyed by sin. Finally, the scene of the Last Supper on the paten depicts the high priest in the act of establishing the New Testament. The chalice should be seen as an object of living faith, with the visual element alluding to the spiritual reality of the religious content.

TWO-HANDLED VASE OF ROCK CRYSTAL
Southern Italian, first half of the 13th century
Rock crystal, mount Vienna, 18th century, height 40.5 cm, diameter 31 cm
Inv. No. KK 2316

ROCK CRYSTAL JUG
Paris, first half of the 14th century
Rock crystal, height 26.3 cm, diameter 17.5 cm
Inv. No. KK 2272

Among the glories of the mediaeval collection is a group of masterpieces of carving in stone. Opinions differ widely about the origin and dating of the faceted monolithic rock crystal vessels with handles carved out of solid stone, because our knowledge of the history

of the design and cutting techniques
involved does not give us any secure
criteria for making judgments. A more
or less continuous tradition in this technically demanding, time-consuming but
truly noble art going back to late antiquity existed only in Constantinople.
The revival of classical stone carving in
the West may be connected with the
conquest of Constantinople in 1204,
when not only a host of art treasures
but also many artists moved West, in
some cases no doubt including the
entire workforces of stone-working
shops. The very earliest guild rulebooks
(1259 Paris, 1284 Venice) distinguished
between two branches: the *arte minuta*
or *subtile* of the gem cutters (lapidaries)
and the *arte grossa,* which comprised
those who produced hollow vessels
from hard stone. Venice had privileged
access to the best pieces of oriental raw
materials. How-ever, we may assume
that a keen stone connoisseur such as
Emperor Frederick II, who is known to
have had good relations with the Islamic
world, had no difficulty in obtaining the
best of the best for the royal workshops
of the Norman and Hohenstaufen court
in Southern Italy and Sicily. However,
stone-cutting and carving as branches
of Frederick II's court art are documen-
tarily supported with securely attributed
works only in the case of cameos.
The large double-handled vase weighs
12.8 kg (28 lbs) and is without compare.
Even the dimensions of the rough block
of quartz must have been impressive,
although its purity right through, which
is marred by very few veins, can only
have become evident when the work
was quite far advanced. The solid block
character of the raw stone is retained in
the tectonically designed outline that
determines the relationship between
the austere crystalline handle shape
and the swelling curves of the vessel.
If we use as our guide the principal
criteria for judging hollow vessels –
the purity of the crystal, the beauty of

the outline and the precision of the cut,
then the single-handled jug of clearest
crystal, which is cut with masterly precision in an elegantly curved outline, is
among the most brilliant achievements
of *arte grossa* anywhere. Its curved
E-shaped handle is considered to be
the most graceful and at the same time
most complex formal solution of the
late mediaeval period. No other hollow
vessel of the time attained the same
perfection, without the least irregularity
in the cut. The attribution of the jug
to French fourteenth-century court art
is finding increasing favour. Vessels of
this kind adorned princely tables and
sideboards. French queens presented
similar luxury articles to princes of the
blood.

KRUMAU MADONNA
Prague, *c.* 1390/1400
Calcareous sandstone,
originally painted
(mantle: white on the
outside, blue inside), with
gilt hair and fringes of robe,
height 112 cm
Inv. No. KK 10156

The Madonna comes from Český Krumlov (Krumau) in southern Bohemia, but stylistically it is a product of Prague court art. This type of Virgin figure with a specific emotional expression is known as a "Beautiful Madonna", and represents an example of the "Soft Style", the south-eastern variant of the International Gothic style in its most delicate form. "Beautiful Madonnas" are one of the finest achievements of court art around 1400. Movingly beautiful, they are idealised manifestations of perfect delicacy and grace. In the happiness of motherhood (which was originally illustrated by her reaching out for the apple in the child's missing right hand), the Virgin presents her Son as the Saviour.

The rhythmic sweep of the curtain of drapery that conceals the body creates a three-dimensional effect on the prominent viewing side with its shadows – lateral cascades of folds frame the deep cavities between the ridges of the folds. The pronounced hollows and undercarving in the ample robe manifest a specific softness. This is evident not only in the flowing linearity of the hems; the undulating surfaces and delicately modelled masses bring out even more prominently the characteristics that give the "Soft Style" its name.

AMETHYST BOWL
Venice, late 14th or early 15th century
Amethyst, mount: gilt silver, height 16.3 cm,
width 23.8 cm
Inv. No. KK 86

The vessel is a typical late-mediaeval
navicula (incense boat), although the
hinged lid has been lost. The setting
with the pomegranate motif and traces
of enamel enable us to identify it as
Venetian and give a rough dating. It is
evidence of the close collaboration
between goldsmiths and *pietra dura*
workers, who around the mid-13th century set up a fraternity of *cristalleri*.
Venice soon emerged as the leading
centre of *pietra dura* work, with most

of its output being exported. Etymolo-
gically, the Greek word "amethyst"
("amethyein" = protect from drunken-
ness) gave the stone a reputation
for protection and warding off evil
thoughts.

"WIENER MUSTERBUCH"
(VIENNESE MODEL BOOK)
Bohemian, 1st quarter of the
15th century
56 colour-highlighted silverpoint
drawings on paper in groups of four on
maple panels, leather case,
each height 9.5 cm, width 9 cm
Inv. Nos. KK 5003 and KK 5004

Model books were functional aids for
workshops and itinerant artists, providing a ready supply of motifs and patterns. In this luxury edition, a painter
working in the "Soft Style" (International Gothic) set out to reproduce the
essence of his source patterns broken
down into motifs. This is the purest
example of a collection of model patterns specialising in various types of
human head and animal skulls. Except
for two later portraits, all the silverpoint
drawings were drawn by one and the
same hand and modelled with a fine

brush in red and white. Its compilation as a folding book and the precious leather case suggest it was a present for an exalted patron from whom the artist may have hoped to obtain commissions.

COVERED ROCK CRYSTAL GOBLET ("HERBERSTEIN GOBLET")

Burgundy or Venice (?), 1st half of the 15th century; mount: Nuremberg (?), 1449, and Graz (?), 1564
Rock crystal, gilt silver, height 25 cm
Inv. No. KK 6896

ROCK CRYSTAL DOUBLE HEAD

Venice, mid-15th century (?); mount: Nuremberg, mid-15th century
Rock crystal, gilt silver, Nuremberg hallmark, partly enamelled, height 24.5 cm
Inv. No. KK 82

The provenance of these two rock-crystal vessels is uncertain. Both Venice and Burgundy have been suggested as possible places of origin. The covered goblet is based on high-mediaeval, two-handled jugs (cf. the jug, Inv. No. 2272). The lenses cut into the body of the vessel in many places appear in similar form on the court goblet once belonging to Duke Philip the Good of Burgundy and now in the Vienna Treasury. The ownership mark and date 1449 on the foot of the goblet indicate that this ornate piece was the property of Emperor Frederick III. It was inherited by Maximilian I and then by Emperor Ferdinand I, who in 1564 bequeathed it to his Graz-based son Archduke Charles II of Inner Austria. The latter gave it the same year to his chamberlain Caspar, Baron von Herberstein, stipulating that the goblet should always be inherited through the male line. The gift and the condition associated with it are recorded in the inscription on the upper mounting of the vessel

which was added on the top right in 1564. The knob carries the arms of the archduke. The rock crystal parts of the double-headed second vessel are possibly much older than the mount, which is mid-fifteenth century. The Nuremberg hallmark provides a secure geographical attribution for the goldwork at least.

EPERGNE WITH "ADDER'S TONGUES"
German, mid-15th century
Gilt silver, fossilised shark's teeth, citrine, height 27 cm
Inv. No. KK 89

It was thought that the fossilised shark's teeth were the tongues of adders (dragons), and they were ascribed the capacity to neutralise poisons in food and drink. Princes had special table holders designed for the coveted "adder's tongues". The shark's teeth were suspended from a little tree like fruit.

On top of a conventional stand, a plant tuft rises from the leaf-covered knob from which sprouts a ring of "adder's tongues". In the middle is a citrine. Two of three surviving tongue-stone holders are in Viennese treasuries, while others are listed as belonging to Frederick III in Vienna and the Duke of Burgundy.

"HOFÄMTERSPIEL" (GAME OF CARDS)

Vienna (?), c. 1455
Complete with 48 surviving cards;
layers of paper, woodcut, watercolour and
opaque colours, gold and silver overlays,
pen drawing, each approx. height 14 cm,
width 10 cm
Inv. Nos. KK 5077 – KK 5124

The game is structured into four armorial
colours (Bohemia, Holy Roman Empire,
France, Hungary) with the help of figurative images in which the hierarchical
structure at court is reflected. All values
are governed by the order of precedence
at court; the court functions include not
only the high court offices occupied by
noblemen but also suppliers and court
servants. Along with a designated office,
each card also has a value given in
Roman numerals. Unique as secular
woodcut images, this card game can
only have been intended to while away
royal hours of leisure. The virtuosity of
the woodcutting skill is unsurpassed –
the lines create an impression of fluid
drawing – and the colour finish is executed with great meticulousness using
gold and silver leaf, the costly effect of
which further heightens the effect of the
engraving. A number of factors suggest
that the client involved was Ladislaus
Postumus (†1457), King of Hungary and
Bohemia and Duke of Austria.

IPPOLITA MARIA SFORZA OR ISABELLA OF ARAGON

Francesco Laurana
(Vrana, c. 1430 – 1502 Avignon)
Naples, c. 1475 or 1488 (?)
Marble, painted, height 44 cm
Inv. No. KK 3405

The Dalmatian artist Francesco Laurana
was one of the great itinerant artists of
the Early Italian Renaissance.
He probably created this bust during
his third visit to Naples. It depicts perhaps Ippolita Maria Sforza, the wife of
King Alfonso of Naples, or her daughter
Isabella, who married Gian Galeazzo
Sforza, Duke of Milan, in 1489. Laurana
adopted a distinctly stylised approach

using simple, smooth rounded shapes, and then breathed life into it using coloured wax. Even the red flowers in the mesh of the gold hair net are modelled in wax, while a real jewel is missing from the attractive lady's forehead. None of the polychroming has survived on any of Laurana's other portraits.

BELLEROPHON TAMING PEGASUS

Bertoldo di Giovanni (model)
(Florence c. 1440–1491 Poggio a Caiano)
Adriano Fiorentino (cast)
(Florence c. 1450/60–1499 Florence)
Florence, c. 1480
Bronze, height 32.5 cm
Inv. No. KK 5596

With the help of Pallas Athene, Bellerophon succeeded in taming Pegasus, the winged horse who served Zeus and who had sprung from the body of Medusa when she was beheaded by Perseus. Borne by Pegasus, Bellerophon carried out numerous heroic deeds, but when he set out to conquer Olympus, the horse threw him off and he went

mad. Bellerophon thus became a symbol of unbridled ambition and hubris leading to downfall. The signature on the underside of the base names both artists, the sculptor and the bronze founder ("EXPRESSIT ME BERThOLDVS CONFLAVIT HADRIANUS") – a rare example at this date. Bertoldo's source was a detail from a Roman sarcophagus relief and the antique Dioscuri statues, which still stood on Monte Cavallo on the Quirinale in Rome. This work was one of the first free-standing bronze statuettes of the Renaissance. As a pupil of Donatello and teacher of Michelangelo, Bertoldo is regarded as a key link between the Early and High Renaissance, which was in part due to his particularly close links with the Medicis.

VIRGIN AND CHILD

Tilman Riemenschneider

(Osterode/Harz c. 1460 –1531 Würzburg)
Würzburg, c. 1495
Limewood with old colouring,
height 145 cm
Inv. No. KK 8899

Riemenschneider's religious beliefs and his own notion of the high quality of his works as autonomous works of art were already visible in his early work, which includes this statue of the Virgin from around 1495. His sculpture encourages reverent meditative contemplation but never runs the risk of encouraging confusion between the reality of the statue and the allusion to the message of redemption that it conveys. In sacrificing individuality – the faces of the Virgin and her Child are based on certain bourgeois types – Riemenschneider was aiming at a general validity that corresponds to the sublimation of expression. The figure was designed with frontal viewing in mind, and within this constraint the sculptor exploits the qualities of the mature wood to the utmost.

CARDINAL GRANVELLA'S VENUS

North Italian, c. 1500
Bronze, silver, height 18.5 cm
Inv. No. KK 7343

This *Venus* was owned by Cardinal Antoine Perrenot de Granvella. Emperor Rudolf II acquired the statue from the cardinal's nephew, Count Cantecroy, in 1600. At the time, it was considered a celebrated work of antiquity, an unusual feature being the silver feet standing out from the green bronze patina. Granvella had the figure mounted on a silver pedestal hallmarked Besançon; Rudolf II kept it in a gilt case. The statuette is a Renaissance-period fake classical piece which however until 1919 was so successful that it was assumed to be genuine.

ALLEGORY OF VANITAS (TRANSIENCE)

Gregor Erhart

(Ulm c. 1470 –1540 Augsburg)

Hans Holbein the Elder (attrib., colouring)

(Augsburg c. 1465 –1524 Augsburg)
Augsburg, c. 1500
Limewood with old painting,
height 46 cm
Inv. No. KK 1

Usually composed as a three-figure group, the image contrasts thematically youth and beauty with age, embodied in the figures of the youth and the girl

vis-à-vis the old woman, whose physical decline is all too clearly evident. The modesty of the approaching young couple contrasts vividly with the shameless revelation of ugliness in the 'horrible beldame', who is a travesty. The moralising intent – with the allusion to the transience of everything mortal – goes hand in hand with a certain pleasure-hating puritanism. The classical world's uninhibited approach to the nude had yet to be regained. The enamel-style glaze and surface richness in the colouring are reminiscent of Holbein the Elder.

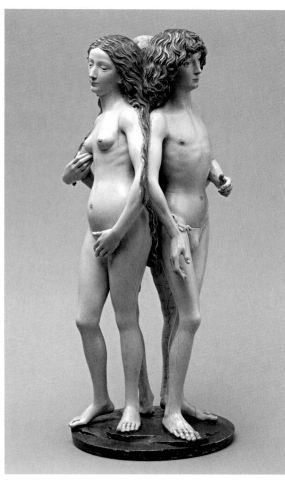

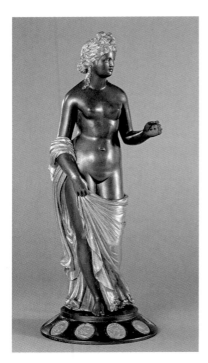

also outstanding for the extraordinary quality of the modelling, cast, chasing, gilding and patina.

YOUNG COUPLE

Tullio Lombardo

(first documented 1475–1532 Venice)
Venice, c. 1500/10
Marble, height 56 cm, width 71.5 cm, depth 20 cm
Inv. No. KK 7471

The notable feature of this relief and a similar one in the Ca' d'Oro in Venice is that in each case the double portrait of a young couple appears to be placed against a neutral background on a narrow baseplate. There were antecedents for this in classical tomb sculpture and the double-portrait type derived from painting north of the Alps that was also adopted by Venetian painters in the early sixteenth century. Inspiration may also have come from Francesco Colonna's

VENUS FELIX

Jacopo Alari-Bonacolsi (Antico)

(Mantua c. 1460–1528 Gazzuolo)
Mantua, c. 1500
Bronze, partly fire gilt; base: limewood with inlaid Roman coins, height 29.8 cm (without base)
Inv. No. KK 5726

The statuette is a free reworking of an antique marble sculpture found in Rome in the late 15th century and placed in the Belvedere Court at the Vatican before 1509 on the instructions of Pope Julius II. Antico was in Rome several times as a restorer of antique figures and purchaser and copyist of classical antiquities for the Gonzagas. When he executed his bronze reductions based on monumental marble sculptures, he did not merely copy them but frequently made good the missing bits of the often only fragmentary originals. Like all bronzes that Antico executed for Bishop Ludovico Gonzaga of Mantua around 1500, this Venus is

allegorical love story Hypnerotomachia Polyphili, published in Venice in 1499. There are often conspicuous parallels between his woodcut illustrations and the works of Tullio Lombardo, who was Venice's leading sculptor around 1500. His reliefs introduced a poetically transfigured mood into sculpture, an achievement that is comparable with Giorgione's in painting. The virtuosity of his technique enabled him to create here ideal

portraits of remarkable vitality, while the fragmentation challenges this illusion. The couple are transformed into busts inspired by classical antiquity, generating a sophisticated intermeshing of various layers of meaning.

DÜRER GOBLET AND MAXIMILIAN GOBLET
Nuremberg, c. 1500 and 1510
Gilt silver, height 47.5 cm
Inv. No. KK 109
Silver, partly gilt, height 56 cm
Inv. No. K 110

Covered goblets were one of the principal products of German goldsmiths' work in the late-Gothic and Renaissance periods. As Dürer's sketchbooks, paintings and engravings show, the great Nuremberg-based master was also fascinated by the design of this traditional mediaeval type of vessel. The goldsmiths probably made pieces from Dürer's designs. Among the surviving works that particularly support that assumption are the "Dürer" goblet and the

"Maximilian" goblet owned by Emperor Maximilian I. The "Dürer" goblet was probably purchased from the estate of Count Montfort-Werdenberg by Archduke Ferdinand II of Tyrol, because the fur-clad "wild man" on the knob of the lid holds the arms of the count's family. The complicated design and yet apparent naturalness of the lid is a further evolution of late-Gothic solutions and was probably developed by Dürer. The characteristic motif of the triple-boss cluster is also found in a goblet in Dürer's Dresden sketchbook. The design of the "Maximilian" goblet, dated ten years later, already exhibits Renaissance characteristics. Instead of the bosses, naturalistic-looking pears rise from the sides of the vessel. On the lid of the goblet is a bough bearing pomegranates, the symbol of a ruler's virtue, while the interior displays the arms of Maximilian I.

TRIUMPHS OF PETRARCH:
THE TRIUMPH OF FAME OVER DEATH

French, early 16th century
Wool, silk, height 428 cm, width 585 cm
Inv. No. T CII/4

The six-part tapestry series is based on the allegorical poem *Trionfi* by the Italian poet and scholar Petrarch (1304–1374), which describes the triumphs of Love, Chastity, Death, Fame, Time and Eternity. The scene shown here is about the triumph of Fame over Death. Winged Fama stands on a triumphal chariot approaching from the left drawn by two white elephants, dressed in a robe of feathers with numerous tongues attached to it. She trumpets the fame of her entourage in all directions. In front of the chariot a cock and a bat can be discerned, symbols of day and night and at the same time harbingers of Fame. The personalities accompanying Fame's chariot are figures from history and literature mentioned by Petrarch – Plato, Alexander, Aristotle, Home, Cicero, Virgil and Charlemagne. They are each labelled with an inscription on the tapestry.

Stylistically, the tapestry represents a transition between two periods. In the foreground is a flat *millefleurs* motif still in a late-Gothic style, while in the background we see a landscape scene in perspective, which is already in a Renaissance vein.

SCOURGING OF CHRIST

Moderno (Galeazzo Mondella)
(Verona 1467–1528 Verona)
Rome, *c.*1506/09
Silver, fire gilt, height 13.8 cm,
width 10.2 cm
Inv. No. KK 1105

The figure of Christ being scourged is based on *Laocoön*, which was dug up in Rome in 1506, while the two ruffians can be traced back to the tyrannicide figures placed in the courtyard at the Palazzo Madama in Rome in the early sixteenth century. However, it was not just for formal reasons that the artist chose these ancient figures as models for his composition. There were good thematic reasons as well. Pliny the Elder for example described the *Laocoön* group as an *exemplum doloris*, as an exemplary presentation of pain. Even the Counter-Reformation, which was generally rather hostile to antiquity, advised artists to use *Laocoön* as a model in depicting the suffering Christ.

ENTHRONED MADONNA AND CHILD ON A CRESCENT MOON

Attributed to Niklaus Weckmann

(Named as burgher 1481–1526)
Ulm, c. 1510
Limewood, with original polychrome
colouring, height 113 cm, width 90 cm,
depth 20 cm
Inv. No. KK 30

The enthroned *Madonna and Child* is thought to have come from a monastery church in Ulm, where it must have formed part of a larger shrine group. Basically a flat box casing, the shrine formed the centrepiece of a winged altar, one of the most impressive forms of late-Gothic art, due in no small part to the skills of the wood carvers of the time. Down to waist level, the figure of the Virgin is carved three-quarters in the round, but below that the body vanishes in spreading drapery in high relief. Instead of statuesque calmness, the work becomes a busy mass of folds and creases. The carved throne – more of a relief-like suggestion of a throne than an actual piece of furniture – and the crescent moon enclose the figured group and round the picture off.

HERCULES AND ANTAEUS

Jacopo Alari-Bonacolsi (Antico)

(Mantua c. 1460–1528 Gazzuolo)
Mantua, c. 1519
Bronze, height 43.2 cm (with base)
Inv. no. KK 5767

The inscription included on the underside of the cast base, "D/ISABEL/LA/ME MAR.", indicates that the bronze belonged to Isabella d'Este, Margravine of Mantua. In response to her request, Antico had agreed to make replicas of a number of models in his possession that he had already cast once, including the reduction of the *Hercules and Antaeus* group now in Florence, which Antico had seen as a torso in Rome. The bronze is his proposal for completing it. The letter also bears out Antico's importance as a pioneer in refining casting techniques that only the duplication of a model made possible.

ADAM AND EVE

Conrat Meit

(Worms c. 1475/80–1550/51 Antwerp)
Mechelen, c. 1520
Beechwood, height 25.5 cm and 24 cm
Inv. Nos. KK 9888 and KK 9889

Conrat Meit worked from 1512 in Mechelen in the service of Archduchess Margaret, stadtholder of the Netherlands. Dürer said he had never seen his equal as a wood carver; although the influence of Dürer's canons of proportion is unmistakable in the figures as ideal shapes, the carver's close attention to the functioning and structure of the body was turned into a creative picture of intense lifelikeness without the fluidity of the movement depicted being thereby in the least impaired.

ST. MICHAEL GOBLET

Antwerp, 1532
Gold, partly enamelled, diamonds,
emeralds, rubies, pearls, height 51.7 cm
Inv. No. KK 1120

This lidded goblet impresses not only by
the quality and variety of the materials
used but also because of the elegance
of its complex shape. The tall, narrow
foot is surmounted by a slender bowl
with frieze-like reliefs of erotic bac-
chante scenes and delicate suspended
garlands between mascarons and
bucranes with pearls dangling from
them. The cup was included with three
other valuable works of art sent by
Charles IX of France to Archduke
Ferdinand of Tyrol in 1570, when the
latter represented the king during his
marriage to Archduchess Elizabeth in
Speyer. Richly set with diamonds, the
little figure of the Archangel Michael
may refer to the French Order of
St. Michael.

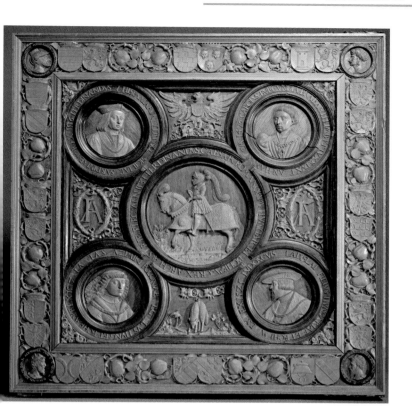

TRICTRAC BOARD AND PIECES

Hans Kels the Elder
(Kaufbeuren c. 1480–1559/60 Kaufbeuren
Kaufbeuren, 1537
Oak, walnut, jacaranda, mahogany,
rosewood; hinges: bronze, height 56 cm,
width 56 cm
Inv. No. KK 3419

The playing surface is made of two
hinged wooden boards that can be folded together. The outsides have a systematic genealogical and heraldic programme glorifying Emperor Charles V
and his brother King Ferdinand I (emper-
or from 1558). The side depicted shows
in the middle an equestrian portrait of
Ferdinand I, probably also the owner of
the board, surrounded by four medallions. Carved in fine miniatures top and
bottom left are the youthful portraits of
his maternal grandfather, Ferdinand the
Catholic, and his father-in-law King

Ladislas of Poland. At the top right is the
portrait of his maternal great-grandfather
Charles the Bold, and below that of his
brother-in-law King Louis of Hungary. In
the small corner medallions are the rulers
of the four great world monarchies: Ninus
of Assyria, Cyrus of Persia, Alexander the
Great of Greece and Romulus, the founder
of Rome. The "AF" monogram relates
to Ferdinand and his wife Anne. On each
inner side of the board, the six object
shapes needed to play trictrac are shown
in expensive inlay work. The border of the
playing board takes the form of exquisite
carved tendril decoration with birds and
beasts plus medallions with mythological
scenes of the moralising kind favoured by
Boccaccio. They relate to the illustrations
on the 32 playing pieces. The board was
possibly designed by Augsburg-based
Jörg Breu the Elder (c. 1475–1537) or his
similarly named son (1510–1547).

SALT CELLAR (SALIERA)

Benvenuto Cellini

(Florence 1500–1572 Florence)
Paris, 1540–1543
Gold, partially enamelled, base: ebony,
height 26 cm, width 33.5 cm
Inv. No. KK 881

The *Saliera* is Cellini's only surviving,
fully authenticated work in gold. It was
commissioned by François I during the
artist's stay in Paris in 1540–1543 and was
subsequently given by Charles IX to
Ferdinand II of Tyrol when the latter represented the king at his wedding with
Archduchess Elizabeth in 1570. This extraordinarily valuable table utensil, which
according to his own account Cellini
wrought freehand from rolled gold, is
also an allegorical representation of the
planet Earth. In his autobiographical
account of his career, he says:
"[…] to show how the Sea is combined
with the Earth, I made two figures a
good palm high sitting next to each
other with intertwined feet, just as we
see the arms of the Sea running into the
Earth. The Sea, depicted as a man, held
a richly wrought ship that could hold
sufficient salt, with four seahorses under
it and the figure holding a trident in
his right hand. I showed Earth as a
woman, with such a beautiful figure
and as graceful as I knew how. Beside
her I placed a rich, decorated temple
on the ground to hold pepper.
[…] On its side were pictures of the
comeliest animals that the Earth could
bring forth." On the throat of the base,
this allegory is completed by the figures
of the four winds, the times of the
day and emblems of human activity.

CHARLES V

Leone Leoni
(Arezzo 1509–1590 Milan)
Milan, 1555
Bronze, height 113 cm
Inv. No. KK 5504

The striking figure of the bust rises from a base shaped as an eagle and two naked human supporting figures, presumably Hercules and Minerva. It represents a conscious borrowing from Roman imperial busts. However, the emperor wears contemporary armour, specifically the suit he wore in 1547 at the Battle of Mühlberg (now in the Armería in Madrid). Leone Leoni produced the bust for Cardinal Granvella, the emperor's chancellor, and Emperor Rudolf II purchased it from his estate in 1600. It then acted in turn as a model for Adriaen de Vries's representational portrait of Rudolf II dated 1603.

KING PHILIP II OF SPAIN

Pompeo Leoni (head)
(Venice [?] c. 1533–1608 Madrid)
Madrid, c. 1556

Balthasar Moll (bust)
(Innsbruck 1717–1785 Vienna)
Vienna, 1753
Head: painted silver, bust: painted terracotta, height 62 cm
Inv. No. KK 3412

The naturalistically painted head of cast silver was presumably enclosed within the king's suit of armour, which reinforced the lifelike quality of the portrait and heightened the immediate presence of the subject, which came close to that of wax portraits.
This situation lasted only until 1753 at the latest, when Balthasar Moll was commissioned to adapt a bust of clay to the head for exhibition in the Treasury. Pompeo Leoni worked for Cardinal Granvella from 1551, and it was through Granvella's offices that he went to Spain instead of his father Leone. The portrait probably dates from around 1556, when Philip II became king.

Overall, however, the decorative style is international and is difficult to localise conclusively.

DRAGON BOWL WITH HANDLE

Gasparo Miseroni

(Milan, *c.* 1518 – 1573 Milan)
Milan, *c.* 1565/70
Lapis lazuli, setting: gold, enamel, emeralds, rubies, pearls, garnets,
height 17 cm, length 18.9 cm
Inv. No. KK 1851

This ornate bowl called on the skills of both the stone cutter and the goldsmith. The result was an image of menacing fantasy: a dragon with glowing ruby eyes opens wide his jaws, arching his long, curved neck as he does so – the beast seems ready to strike.
His wings span forwards to grasp the back of the vessel. The body of the dragon is continued in flat relief on the sides of the bowl, dividing into two spiralling flipper-like feet. Dragon motifs of this kind were typical of Miseroni's

"MERCURY GOBLET"

Netherlands or Spain, *c.* 1560
Gold, partly enamelled, emeralds,
height 34.4 cm
Inv. No. KK 1095

The embossed goblet of beaten gold stands on three opened pomegranates, whose seeds take the form of rubies. Mercury stands on the low embossed lid as a handle, holding up an enamelled ring with a large emerald. The rows of bosses on the side of the goblet and the lid are set with elaborately worked bands consisting of enamelled beading and lily motifs with rubies and emeralds in surrounded by a square frame.
The shape of the vessel and the pomegranate feet derive from late-Gothic gold work. The contrast between the smoothness of the overall shape and the filigree detail was particularly characteristic of Netherlandish/Spanish taste in the mid-sixteenth century.

workshop in Milan. The demonic beast finally becomes grotesque ornamentation in the form of a stylised volute motif and the mask under the handle. The piece comes from Emperor Rudolf II's collection.

CABINET

Giovanni Battista Serabaglio
(mentioned in Milan in 1560)

Marco Antonio Fava
(mentioned in Milan in 1560)

Giuseppe de Vico
(mentioned 1567–1576)
Milan, 1567
Wrought iron, fire gilt, damascened in gold and silver, coloured blue, etched, engraved, bronze, wood, partly painted, height 90.5, length 47.5 cm, width 68.5 cm
Inv. No. KK 879

The expensively decorated tempietto-shape iron casing, the front of which can be folded forward as a flap, opens to reveal a small rectangular wooden chest with 53 drawers for the storing of valuables. Stylistic considerations suggest that it is the work of the Milan-based armourer Giovanni Battista Serabaglio and the goldsmith Marco Antonio Fava. The bronze statuettes added later and inscribed "JOSEF DE VICO FECIT 1567" are in line with the complex programme of allegorical scenes of rulers in the form of Virtues, Muses and classical deities, and indicate that the owner was a person of high status, probably Emperor Maximilian II. There are related objects in Paris, Milan and London.

BEZOAR
Spanish, 3rd quarter of the 16th century
Gold, emeralds, rubies, height 25.5 cm
Inv. No. KK 981

The word "bezoar" comes from the Persian term *bâd-sahr* = antidote. The stone is formed in the stomach or intestine of certain ruminants, and until the eighteenth century was considered an effective remedy against various ailments such as melancholy and epilepsy. As the name says, it was also seen as a mysterious antidote for poisoning. Because of these therapeutic qualities, it was customary for bezoars to be particularly carefully preserved and, expensively set, given to princes as presents. This bezoar is set on a gold ring borne by three ornamental lions. Four emerald-studded bands together with dragon-style volutes enclose the stone. A crown, similarly studded with emeralds, completes the structure at the top.

OSTRICH EGG CUP
Clement Kicklinger
(Master 1561–1617 in Augsburg)
Augsburg, c. 1570/75
Ostrich egg, coral, gilt/painted silver,
height 56.8 cm
Inv. No. KK 897

The combination of exotic *naturalia* and refined gold work makes this cup a typical Kunstkammer or Wunderkammer piece. On top of a pierced base with sturdy coral trunks, a Moor leads an ostrich on a long chain, the bird carrying its own egg on its back. It also has a horseshoe in its beak, which even in the sixteenth century was a bringer of luck. The motif of ostriches as eaters of iron derives from classical legend, and means "strength through resistance", because the bird is so robust that it can digest stone and iron and draw nourishment from them. The corals are complementary, because they were considered to be a remedy against lumps in the intestines and the blood as well as providing protection against the evil eye and magic.

ASTRONOMY

**Jean Boulogne,
called Giambologna**
(Douai 1529–1608 Florence)
Florence, c. 1573
Bronze, fire gilt, height 38.8 cm
Inv. No. KK 5893

The young woman depicted in the statuette is an allegory of Astronomy, as the attributes of a prism, armillary sphere, spirit level, ruler, compasses and plumb line indicate. In old inventories she was therefore listed as *Venus Urania*.

The statuette represents a high point in Giambologna's efforts to show a beautiful naked female body from an infinite number of equally perfect angles, that is "equally beautiful from all sides". The work dates from c. 1573, probably the time when the artist was executing his *Apollo* statuette for the *studiolo* of Francesco de' Medici, with which it forms a compositional pair.

TWO-FIGURE RAPTUS GROUP

Jean Boulogne, called Giambologna
(Douai 1529–1608 Florence)
Antonio Susini
(1558–1624 Florence)
Florence, c. 1580
Bronze, height 98.2 cm
Inv. No. KK 6029

In this composition it is not a historical topic which is being shown – what Bologna was interested in was simply the formal problem of a multi-figure group in extreme motion in which a male figure lifts a walking female figure. The two-figure composition is thus the beginning of a development that would culminate in the famous three-figure

marble group of the *Rape of the Sabine Women,* unveiled in 1583. Giambologna sent a first version of the two-figure group (now in Naples) to Ottavio Farnese. The Viennese version shows a auter and more dynamic composition. he perfect execution can probably be scribed to Antonio Susini.

MERCURY

Jean Boulogne, called Giambologna
(Douai 1529 – 1608 Florence)
Florence, *c.* 1585
Bronze, height 62.7 cm
Inv. No. KK 5898

Mercury is shown here in flight – in other words, Giambologna was abandoning the laws of statics that governed sculpture to move into a type of image previously the preserve of painting and painting-like reliefs. As the messenger of the gods and executor of Jupiter's instructions, Mercury points with his raised right hand to the source of all wisdom. It was a subject that Giambologna had become interested in during his stay in Bologna in 1563. In 1565, Cosimo de' Medici sent a roughly life-size bronze statue of Mercury to Emperor Maximilian II, which is perhaps preserved in Stockholm. Compositionally the most mature solution is found in the signed statuette in Vienna, which comes from Emperor Rudolf's *Kunstkammer*.

TABLE CLOCK
Gross Family (case)
David Altenstetter (basse taille enamel)
(Colmar *c.* 1547–1617 Augsburg)
Augsburg, *c.* 1585
Silver, partly gilt, enamel, movement, iron, brass, height 21.8 cm
Inv. No. KK 1121

Princes also commissioned selected works from outstanding masters in the guilds of the imperial cities. The workmanship they produced was way above average, but they mostly contented themselves with turning out standard types of product. Imperial cities such as Augsburg and Nuremberg were responsible for Germany's leading role in building mechanical instruments. Translucent basse taille enamel covers all surfaces of the housing. Even the corner pillars that carry the polygonal upper part terminating in a flat dome are decorated with a gleaming, jewel-like decoration of grotesques, tendrils and animals. The richness of the clock bears witness to the preciousness of time. We observe a new feeling for the value of time surfacing.

LARGE HERON-SHAPED CENTREPIECE

Saracchi workshop

Milan, c. 1590
Rock crystal; mounting: gold, enamel,
precious stones, gems, pearls,
height 39.4 cm
Inv. No. KK 2401

In their quest for a design that could
give the *cristalleri* (rock crystal cutters)
a chance to show off their pictorial
talents, the Saracchi developed vessels
in the shape of animals. In these bird-
shaped centrepieces, called *Raiger*
(German: *Reiher*, herons) in old inventories, Giovanni Ambrogio Saraccho was
generally responsible for the carving
and grinding. His brother Simone executed the fine inlays in the sides. All the
animal features are concentrated in the
top part of the vessel. Below the shoulder line, the shape becomes stylised,
with incised pictorial and ornamental
decoration. Real heron feathers dangling
diagonally backwards from the head
formerly emphasized the heron shape
suggested by the outline.

TABLE AUTOMATON WITH DIANA ON THE CENTAUR

Hans Jakob I Bachmann

(active 1598 – 1651)
Augsburg, c. 1598/1600)
Silver, partly gilt, deep-carved enamel,
pearls, garnets, ebony, height 39.5 cm
Inv. No. KK 1166

This outstanding example of Augsburg
gold work around 1600 combines the
function of a clock with that of a table
automaton, here in the shape of a
Trinkspiel (drinking game). A complicated mechanism in the base and belly
of the centaur made by an unknown
clockmaker moves the group across the
table, Diana and one of the hunting
dogs turn their heads, the centaur rolls
his eyes and shoots off an arrow.
The guest in whose direction the
arrow flies has to empty his glass. Diana
the huntress on a stag was one of the

favourite motifs for *Trinkspiele* at this time. By analogy, the huntress riding on the centaur here is also interpreted as Diana.

JASPER JUG

Ottavio Miseroni (jug)
(Milan *c.* 1568–1624 Prague)
Paulus van Vianen (mount)
(Utrecht *c.* 1570–1613 Prague)
Prague, 1590/1600 (mount: 1608)
Jasper, gold, height 35.5 cm
Inv. No. KK 1866

This unique piece appears to have been cast as a whole, but in fact it was made in two sections. Originally the jug did not need a mount. It is a virtuoso monolith piece of work produced by Ottavio Miseroni pre-1600 (Miseroni worked in Prague from 1588). The mount, marked by Paulus van Vianen and dated 1608, was executed when the dragon's head on the handle was redone in a different sort of jasper. A gold drape covers the join. On the lid, a nereid rises from the water and puts the dragon on a chain.

On the base, counterbalancing this gold work, is a broad ring with depictions of the four elements represented by Jupiter (fire), Juno (air), Pluto (earth) and Amphitrite (water). Four ibex heads divide the ring into sections, their horns forming the support.

HOUSE ALTAR WITH CHRIST AND THE SAMARITAN WOMAN

Gian Ambrogio Caroni (frame)
(† 1611 Florence)
Jacques Byliveldt (gold work)
(Delft 1550–1603 Florence)
Bernardino Gaffuri (walls of niche)
(† 1606 Florence)
Cristofano Gaffuri (central area)
(† 1626 Florence)
Florence, completed 1600
Commessi in *pietra dura*, frame: rock crystal
height 37.8 cm, width 23.5 cm
Inv. No. KK 1542

This domestic altar produced for Grand Duke Ferdinando de' Medici is one of the most exquisite treasures ever to have owed its existence to princely patronage. It took a decade to make, and the complex intermeshing of the work of different artists gives a graphic illustration of the close collaboration within the grand ducal court workshops, founded in 1572 and reorganised by Ferdinand I in 1588, as the predecessor of the Opificio delle Pietre Dure which still operates today.
The magnificent, window-like frame of rock crystal, whose austere architectural structure and balanced proportions are as impressive as the brilliant idea of a vase forming the crown of the broken pediment, derives from a design by architect Bernardo Buontalenti.
Gian Ambrogio Caroni, who generally carved vessels, took a year to execute this richly profiled aedicule. In order to accommodate the extraordinarily demanding ambitions of the Grand Duke, in 1591 goldsmith Jacques Byliveldt decorated the long sides of the frame with female herms in gold, also with

ower garlands, festoons, masks and
artouches in gold enamel. This elabo-
ately designed aedicule was listed in a
Medici inventory in 1598 as still lacking
 picture. This was completed two years
ater by Cristofano Gaffuri. It consists of
 three-dimensionally carved figure
roup against a vivid landscape backround.

he scene features Christ and the
amaritan Woman at Jacob's Well. The
atter is carved from a large emerald.
he lining of the architecturally
esigned niche for the figures was exe-
uted a few months later by Cristofano's
rother Bernardino. He used thin gold
dges to separate the individual panels.
Cristofano Gaffuri himself was consid-
red the outstanding man among the
tone carvers, especially for Florentine
mosaics. In the commesso in pietre dure,
he old notion of an indestructible work

of art was realised. The Florentine
masters developed a particular feeling
for making use of both the natural
colour and the naturally evolved interplay of the veins and grain in the stone.
By the sophisticated exploitation of
the stone drawings, they themselves
brought out details of the pictures.
The lower cartouche with the arms of
Emperor Charles VI, the later owner,
was only commissioned by Francis
Stephen of Lorraine, who as ruling
Grand Duke gave the altar to his father-
in-law between 1737 and 1740.

PRASEM BOWL

Jan Vermeyen (mount)
(Brussels pre-1559–1606 Prague)
Workshop of Ottavio Miseroni
(Milan *c.* 1568–1624 Prague)
Prague, *c.* 1600/05
Prasem, gold, partly enamelled, garnets,
citrine, amethyst, hyacinth, height 23.5 cm,
diameter 17.6 cm
Inv. No. KK 1918

In this ornate vessel, it is the goldsmith
who deserves the crown; the stone carver must have followed his design.
The shape of the bowl is thus unique
among the vessels made of precious
stones. Only the extremely thin walls
(1.2–2 mm) indicate that Miseroni himself must have been involved in making
it. The rich design of the lid in particular,
with its heart-shaped, slightly curved
tiles, highlights the extent to which the
stone carver was subject to the goldsmith's design. The top is formed by a
faceted citrine. The numerous garnets,
which are placed in rows inside the bowl,
leave no doubt as to the origins of the
piece in Prague. This is also confirmed
by the details of the gold enamel work,
where the hand of Vermeyen can be
discerned.

TANKARD MADE FROM A NARWHAL TUSK

Jan Vermeyen
(Brussels pre-1559–1606 Prague)
Prague, *c.* 1600/05
Narwhal tusk ('unicorn'), gold enamelled,
diamonds, rubies, double cameo of agate,
height 22.2 cm
Inv. No. KK 1113

The real 'jewel' of this vessel was considered to be the piece of 'unicorn' that
forms the sides. Great therapeutic effects
were ascribed to the horn of the legendary animal, which since 1200 had
been equated with the tusk of the narwhal. According to Anselmus Boetius de
Boodt, a personal physician of Rudolf II,
the unicorn was so highly prized because
nothing surpassed it in identifying, fore-
stalling and countering any kind of poi-
son, so that its price far exceeded that of
gold. That is the measure of the ambition
behind the design of this vessel. Jan Vermeyen, Rudolf II's personal jeweller whom
the emperor had summoned to Prague in
autumn 1597, executed the rich gold
enamelling with precious stones. The fine
double cameo on the lid presumably
comes from Miseroni's workshop in
Milan.

STATE PITCHER

Christoph Jamnitzer
(Nuremberg 1563 – 1618 Nuremberg)
Nuremberg, c. 1601/02 (?)
Gilt silver, enamel, height 43.5 cm
Inv. No. KK 1128

The state jug and state bowl make a set that was taken to coronation ceremonies in Frankfurt purely as a showpiece, even though it was unsuitable for washing purposes. The iconographic source was Petrarch's *Trionfi*, with the triumphal procession of Cupid shown on the basin. On the jug, the sequence of triumphs continues with the triumph of Chastity over Love (unicorns), Death over Chastity (buffalo), Fame over Death (elephants), Time over Fame (stag) and Eternity over Time. The last triumph of the divinity deviates from Petrarch's text, because it involves pagan rather than Christian motifs. In the picture of an assembly of the gods on Olympus, a mythological, emblematically coded programme is included in compressed form: Psyche's admission to Olympus as a parable for the immortality of the soul, the Graces as a metaphor of God's

mercy and the emblem of the *fata homerica*, or "Gates of Jupiter", in which fate takes shape in the vessels, filled with the good and the evil. On top is a Venus on the swan as a symbol of heavenly love.

Christoph Jamnitzer, the product of a great family tradition and distinguished by his experience in Italy, was the towering artistic personality in Nuremberg in the early seventeenth century. He worked as a goldsmith, draughtsman, designer of city hall sculptures, engraver and author of the *Neuw Grotteßken Buch*.

SEYCHELLES NUT PITCHER

Anton Schweinberger (mount)
(Augsburg mid-16th century –1603 Prague)

Nikolaus Pfaff (carving)
(Nuremberg 1556? –1612 Prague)
Prague, 1602
Half Seychelles nut (from the *Lodoica Seychellarum*), silver, partly gilt,
height 38.5 cm
Inv. No. KK 6872

The pitcher is a masterpiece of Prague gold work from Emperor Rudolf II's time. Schweinberger, who had been employed at the Prague court since 1587, went far beyond the conventional task of mounting a rare item of *naturalia*. The nut had been discovered as flotsam in the Maldives, and was considered a marine species. That explains

the use of marine motifs throughout the work. Schweinberger inscribed his sculptural design in a rhombus, the diagonals of which run horizontally along the edge of the nut and vertically through the lateral clasps and the axis of the foot. Fluid transitions smooth over the change of directions. Two tritons sitting back to back support the vessel, with their stooped heads and extended arms shifting the accent to the horizontal of the boat-shaped body. The transition is echoed by the busy group on the lid, which shows Neptune riding on a hippocampus (trident missing). The heavy scrollwork and auricular work of the beak and handle keep the balance n the other two corners of the rhombus. Surfaces alternating between gold and silver enhance the multi-layered effect and at the same time clarify the blurred boundaries between abstraction and figurative design. For example, the auricular changes on the handle on the back into a cowering creature moving across the shoulders of the vessel with ts flippers. Schweinberger succeeded n creating a work of inner monumentality; he created this monument to Neptune, marking it with his full name under the base. The pitcher is the sole surviving work which can definitely be attributed to him; it was also the last work that he completed. With its sheer artistry, this 'setting' goes far beyond what is normally considered craftwork. This is an autonomous work of art for the imperial *Kunstkammer*. The subtle surface reliefs of the nut, which depict pairs of marine deities, were the work of the imperial carver Nikolaus Pfaff.

MARS, VENUS AND CUPID

Hubert Gerhard

(s'Hertogenbosch *c.* 1545/50 – 1620 Munich)
Innsbruck, *c.* 1602/05
Bronze, height 41.4 cm
Inv. No. KK 5848

Like his Netherlandish sculptor colleagues Giambologna, Adriaen de Vries and Johann Gregor van der Schardt, Hubert Gerhard also spent some years studying in Italy. Who taught him is not known, but he is documented as being in Florence in 1581. In the same year, he entered the service of the Fuggers, executing a monumental fountain for their Kirchheim castle (1585–1590), which was topped by a Mars, Venus and Cupid group now in the Bavarian National Museum in Munich. Around 1605, when he was in the service of Archduke Maximilian III in Innsbruck, he went back to the subject, transforming it by means of more elegant, supple proportions into a cabinet item.

EMPEROR RUDOLF II

Adriaen de Vries
(Den Haag *c.* 1545 – 1626 Prague)
Prague, 1603
Bronze, height 112 cm
Inv. No. KK 5506

Adriaen de Vries was court sculptor to Rudolf II in Prague from 1601. This bust was commissioned by the Emperor as a counterpart to that of Charles V by Leone Leoni (see page 101), which Rudolf had acquired only in 1600. It is not only the freer painterly style of modelling that is fascinating.

De Vries surpassed the Leoni piece formally as well by conferring more drama and majestic pathos on the bust by slightly turning the body and raising the gaze, which also sets the viewer at a great distance. He thus achieved a degree of courtly showmanship in the portrait that went far beyond anything previously produced by sculpture, and

which was only surpassed by Bernini's portraits of rulers.

TRIUMPH OF BACCHUS, DRINKING GAME (TRINKSPIEL)

Sylvester II Eberlin (?)

(c. 1570–1639 Augsburg, became master craftsman c. 1604)

Hans Schlottheim (organ works)

(Naumburg/Saale c. 1545–1625 Augsburg)
Augsburg, c. 1605
Gilt silver, remains of colouring;
two mechanisms: iron, brass, height 43 cm, length 53 cm
Inv. No. KK 959

Trinkspiele were among the most endearing inventions of Augsburg's goldsmiths around 1600. This witty Trinkspiel takes the form of a triumphal chariot with a Bacchic group ensconced on the separate upper section. It was commissioned as a table decoration for the court, but soon found its way into Rudolf II's imperial Kunstkammer in Prague. Having a drive mechanism concealed inside the chariot, the ensemble could move of its own accord across the table top. Two satyrs romp on the volutes of the shafts. On top of the richly decorated box-shaped top piece is a youthful Bacchus sitting on an amiable billy goat and accompanied by his friends. The interior contains an organ mechanism the same as the one in the boat automaton and is likewise attributable to Hans Schlottheim. This mechanism also operates the movements of the figures: Bacchus lifts his arm, the parrot beats its wings and the musician picks up his instrument. The reason why the whole top piece can be removed from the chariot is probably so the billy goat can be used as a drinking cup, as befits a Trinkspiel. Its head could be removed so that the people at table could drink the wine poured into it. Even more than the two rollicking young satyrs, it is the bagpipe player squatting top rear dangling his legs that confers a sense of sheer fun on the ensemble.

FURY

"Furienmeister"

Salzburg (?), c. 1610/20
Ivory, height 37,4 cm
Inv. No. KK 3727

The unknown ivory carver who made this statuette has been called the Furienmeister (Master of the Furies). However, the term does highlight the chief features of his style: furioso movement combined with a virtuoso command of expressive values. The figure of the fury reaching out into space is full of wild expression, which is intensified by the elongated, sinewy proportions, fluttering, twisting drapery and deeply undercarved details. The workshop of this outstanding artist has so far not been geographically localised. Salzburg is the most likely location; perhaps it belonged to a sculptor of small figures who occasionally worked in Northern Italy.

MYTHOLOGICAL AND ALLEGORICAL PIECES: DANAE

Francesco Primaticcio (design)
(Bologna 1504–1570 Paris)

Jean and Pierre Le Bries (manufacture)
(active in Fontainebleau presumably
between 1540 and 1550)
Fontainebleau, 1540–1550
Wool and silk, gold and silver thread,
height 332, width 625 cm
Inv. No. T CV/1

The wall tapestry with the scene of
Danae forms part of a six-part series.
The young woman was shut away with
her nurse by her father King Acrisius of
Argos on the Peloponnese, as the oracle
of Delphi had predicted that the king
would meet a violent death at the hands
of his grandson. Zeus evaded Acrisius's
precautions by entering Danae's chamber in the form of a shower of golden
rain, impregnating the lovely Danae
and begetting Perseus.
The series was commissioned by the
French king François I. The pictures were
not based on specially prepared cartoons
but on scenes on the south wall of the
Great Gallery in the château at Fontainebleau. When it was converted into the
medium of textiles, the whole wall context was therefore taken into account.
Each tapestry shows not only the fresco
concerned but also the surrounding
stucco work, the cornice and the start
of the coffered ceiling. This makes the
trompe l'œil effect unique among French
tapestries in the sixteenth century.

RIDING LESSONS: CREATING THE HORSE

Jacob Jordaens (design)
(Antwerp 1593–1678 Antwerp)
C. 1640/50

Everard III. Leyniers (manufacture)
(1597–1680)
Brussels, c. 1650
Wool and silk, some gold and silver thread,
height 410 cm, width 521 cm
Inv. No. T XL/1

The composition of the tapestry from
the Viennese series of riding lessons
illustrates the creation of the horse and
displays a mythological scene based on
the writings of classical authors. In the
centre of the scene, which is based on

a cartoon by Flemish artist Jacob Jordaens, is the sea god Neptune. He is depicted at the moment of creating a mettlesome steed with a powerful thrust of his trident, causing it to rear, whinnying. The shell on which Neptune rides across the sea is flanked by dolphins, nereids and a triton who carries a *buccina,* a spiral shell, as a wind instrument. Neptune has been regarded also as the god of horses ever since antiquity, and according to both Pausanius and Diodorus Siculus he is the patron of riding. No scene could therefore be more appropriate as an introduction for a series of tapestries illustrating the high school of riding than Neptune creating the horse.

CITRINE FLOWER VASE

Dionysio Miseroni

(Prague c. 1607–1661 Prague)
Prague, c. 1647/48
Citrine, agate flowers, jasper, chalcedony,
rock crystal, setting: enamelled gold,
height 26 cm (excluding flowers)
Inv. No. KK 1330

In spring 1623, the ageing Ottavio
Miseroni asked the emperor if he could
employ his son Dionysio, who was in no
way a lesser sculptor, as a paid assistant
in the workshop. Following Ottavio's
death in 1624, Dionysio took over his
father's workshop and even surpassed
him in fame. His carved vessels represent the last flowering of the Prague
school of stone carving. In his vessels,
Dionysio's preferred shapes were oblong
and angular crystal shapes. This monolithic, slightly conical citrine vase, which
the master himself numbered among his
principal works, rises from a regular
hexagon with edges adorned with

sculptured herms. The goldsmith added
satyr heads with delicate siren handles
mounted on them above the facing pair
of herms. Austere pipes are cut into the
base. The particular stone used required
a taxing, compact design of true sculptural quality. The vase cost 6,000 florins.
The flowers – roses, tulips and campanu-
las on coloured silver stems – were executed by imperial gem cutter Paul Pertz.
The idea of bunches of flowers on stones
had already been used in Milanese
works.

TANKARD WITH HUNTING AND FISHING SCENES

Balthasar Griessmann

(Wasserburg c. 1620–1706 Salzburg)
Vienna (?), 3rd quarter of the 17th century
Ivory, height 29.8 cm
Inv. No. KK 4472

Being an admired masterpiece of virtuoso ivory carving, the covered jug was
never intended for ordinary use. Almost
the entire surface of the vessel is broken
up into hunting and fishing scenes based
on Dutch engraved antecedents of the
late sixteenth to mid-seventeenth centuries. Even the fragile handle structure

and spout form part of the scheme. The crowning feature is accordingly putti riding on dolphins. Griessmann probably worked in Vienna and Salzburg. His works are notable for their clear articulation into ornamental parts and figured frieze, as well as the delicate layering combining flat relief, high relief and numerous freely sculptured parts.

ROCK CRYSTAL PYRAMID

Dionysio Miseroni
(Prague *c.* 1607–1661 Prague)
Hanns Reinhardt Taravell (setting)
Prague, *c.* 1651/53
Gilt silver, appliqués: enamelled gold,
height 145.4 cm
Inv. Nos. KK 2251 – KK 2254

This 'pyramid' is Dionysio Miseroni's supreme masterpiece. The massive base block rises on a hexagonal foot – an approximate hexafoil. A row of scales beneath the herm heads frame two visible sides decorated alternately with vine leaves and grapes. Four reducing cylindrical stemmed goblets stand on top of the base section, with a double-eagle lid on top. The maker cut all the top sections out of the large vase, with the broader cylinder in each case coming after the narrower one above in the work process. The technical bravura that made the 'pyramid' one of the top *mirabilia* in the Viennese *Schatzkammer* (Treasury) thus owes its unusual design to its maker's technical virtuosity in the service of art. Not surprisingly, this is the only work he signed and dated.

ALLEGORY OF THE ELEMENTS OF WATER AND AIR

Matthias Steinl

(Mattsee/Salzburg? c. 1643/44 –
1727 Vienna)
Vienna, c. 1688/90
Walrus tusk, height 43.4 cm
Inv. No. KK 4533

Three intertwined sea divinities rise from a base of shells, dolphins and marine creatures – a triton blowing into a shell horn, an almost naked young man carrying a fish on his back and a likewise nearly naked woman carrying a large shell. A putto descends from above beneath an archly curling ribbon to reach for the shell. This is a scene about the elements of water and air coming into contact with each other in the jet of a foaming wave.

The three-dimensionally and spatially rich structure of one of the finest pieces of ivory carving is inimitably composed within the narrow confines of a walrus tusk.

KING JOSEPH I ON HORSEBACK

Matthias Steinl

(Mattsee/Salzburg? c. 1643/44 –
1727 Vienna)
Vienna, 1693
Ivory, height 70.8 cm (with base)
Inv. No. KK 4663

As a counterpart to the equestrian portrait of Emperor Leopold I, the statuette of his 15-year-old son Joseph I is part of an allegorical double monument. The work was probably commissioned for the election and coronation of Joseph I as Holy Roman Emperor on 4th March 1690 and the subsequent triumphal entry of the imperial family into Vienna. With his successor (from 1705), Emperor Leopold was highlighting the present and future of the newly strengthened Austrian dynasty.

Over a lace-decorated tunic Joseph I wears a cuirass with imperial double-eagle device and initials "JI" on the hest. The arms of Hungary (right) and Bohemia (left) are reproduced on the pistol holsters.

Beneath the feet of the rearing horse is Furor (raging madness), defeated by the virtues and strength of the young king. Furor's attributes are snakes, burning torches and 'shackling' by a padlock on the upper right arm.

With the Turkish arrows ground under the back right hoof of the horse, the figure is intended to be seen as a servant of War, but also embodying the powers of Evil. Terrified by the sudden appearance of the rider with fluttering cloak, the enemy retracts his hand. With this work composed of several parts Steinl reached the apogee of his career as a carver.

EMPEROR CHARLES V'S CAMPAIGN TO TUNIS: THE ARMY WITHDRAWS FROM TUNIS. THE IMPERIAL TROOPS MAKE CAMP NEAR RADAS

Jan Cornelisz Vermeyen (design)
(Beverwijck near Haarlem 1490/95–1559 Brussels)

Judocus de Vos (manufacture)
(active between 1700 and 1725)
Brussels, 1712–1721
Wool and silk, some gold and silver thread, height 527 cm, width 890 cm
Inv. No. T X / 7

Emperor Charles V's victorious campaign to Tunis is documented in a series of tapestries now in Madrid. The original-size, reverse-image cartoons required to produce the tapestries now in the *Kunsthistorisches Museum* were produced by the painter Jan Cornelisz Vermeyen from 1546. Vermeyen was present on the campaign in person as a documenting artist, and put particular emphasis on accurately recording the battle sites. The tapestry shown belongs to a ten-part Tunis series commissioned

only in the eighteenth century by Emperor Charles VI, but it was woven from the original cartoons. In the fore-ground of the tapestry, the army gets under way at the emperor's command, enabling the artist to show soldiers pro-cessing past with exotic booty, includ-ing cattle, goats and sheep, but also ostriches and dromedaries. The proces-sion of animals is accompanied by slave girls and soldiers.

MARIA THERESIA'S BREAKFAST SERVICE

Anton Matthias Domanek
(Vienna 1713–1779 Vienna)
Vienna, *c.* 1750
Gold, ebony, porcelain
Inv. Nos. KK 1197 and the following

In a supplementary entry dated 16th January 1781, the *Schatzkammer* inventory for 1773 mentions the accession of the 'gold "night things" of Her Late Royal and Imperial Majesty the Empress' (Maria Theresia), who had died on 29th November 1780. The 'night things' referred to a collection of around 70 objects of heavy gold belonging to two matching sets with different functions – a breakfast service and a toilette set. Of the breakfast service, the illustration shows the teapot, the rechaud with a kettle for hot water, and a pot and a cup for hot chocolate, made of Meissen (Dresden) china with gold trim. There is also a sugar bowl on a cup, a teacup of Chinese porcelain, a spatula and a spoon. The toilette set consists of a mirror, wash bowl and jug, candleholder,

powder box, rock crystal bottles with gold mounts, toothbrushes, razors and the like. The fact that razors were included indicates that the toilette set belonged to Maria Theresia's husband Emperor Franz I. In its stylish elegance and perfect craftsmanship, this double set is one of the most important of its kind, and at the same time one of the outstanding achievements of the Viennese goldsmiths' art in the eighteenth century.

SURTOUT DE TABLE (CENTREPIECE) OF DUKE CHARLES ALEXANDER OF LORRAINE

Pieter Jozef Fonson

(Mons 1713–1799 Brussels)
Brussels, 1755 (additions 1770 and 1794)
Gold, porcelain, height 54.5 cm,
length 63.2 cm, width 46 cm
Inv. Nos. KK 1268 – KK 1280

Maria Theresia's brother-in-law Duke Charles Alexander of Lorraine was a hearty trencherman and therefore had splendid tableware. Of his extensive gold table service, only four candlesticks and two sauceboats plus the centrepiece survive. The central motif is a pierced basket – with a bouquet of no longer original ultra-delicate porcelain flowers inside – standing on a serving-board style tray, supported by four candlesticks. The flowers include several little figures of Chinese porcelain.

Round this central group are pairs of oil and vinegar containers set in gold, two gold sugar sprinklers and four little porcelain containers with lids. The latter are marked with the Viennese escutcheon and the date 1794. Changes were already commissioned in 1770, when Jakob Frans van der Donck (Brussels 1724–1801 Brussels) was commissioned to redesign and add to the ensemble, in which he included older parts of the surtout. It is difficult nowadays to identify Fonson's original work except for the platter right and left of the duke's bearings, signed and dated by him.

Picture Gallery

Ill. on pages 128/129:
Hall XIV.

The Picture Gallery in the *Kunsthistorisches Museum* owes its formation and character to a series of great collectors among the Habsburgs themselves. Despite the radical changes towards a republican, democratic museum policy and the collecting activities of the twentieth century, the Gallery has retained its character as a privileged royal collection. This is probably more obvious here than in other comparable art galleries founded on former royal and princely patronage.

The gallery's character was already determined in principle by around 1800. Despite its diversity and richness, it is an unsystematic collection. It has incomparable strengths, but also serious – indeed astonishing – gaps. Closely associated with countries long under the dominion of the Habsburgs, the painting collection derives its specific character from the art of these regions. Its strengths in quality and quantity come from Germany, the Catholic south of the Netherlands, northern Italy and the Italian and Spanish centres of Baroque painting (Bologna, Naples, Florence, Venice and Madrid). Largely absent are France, England, Protestant Holland (apart from a few major works) and the Italian city-states of the Early Renaissance period.

As powerful rulers, the Habsburgs admired consummate perfection rather than a state of potentially ungainly development. There are few works from early stylistic phases, works striving solely for inner fulfilment, no thirteenth- or fourteenth-century material, scarcely anything of the Italian quattrocentro, no "struggling, brooding types", few sketches. The fondness for portraits noticeable in all royal collections is particularly evident in the Viennese gallery. There was a preference for ripe, indeed over-ripe, styles, for the Venetian and Flemish sixteenth and seventeenth centuries, elaborate, perfect – decorative – pieces. The Gallery itself was seen as a decorative ensemble. Eccentricity was not favoured. The qualities that aroused admiration were seemingly effortless mastery and incontestable elegance. Habsburg taste was orthodox without actually lapsing into bigotry. All the great Habsburg collectors loved Early Netherlandish artists, Bruegel, the Venetians, Dürer, subsequently Rubens and Van Dyck and the grandiose aspect of the Italian Baroque. The rest of the field complied with this taste as best it could.

Above all, there are four groups of acquisitions associated with the Habsburg princes who were primarily responsible for shaping the profile of the Viennese Gallery. Although many of the paintings owned by Emperor Rudolf II were scattered to the four winds after the Swedish sack of Prague in 1648, important pictures had already been moved to Vienna soon after the emperor's death in 1612 and so remained in Habsburg possession. They included the Bruegel collection Rudolf had taken over from his brother Ernst, the Dürer holdings, and the works of Rudolf's court painters in Prague. These and a series of masterpieces of Italian Mannerism (Correggio, Parmigianino) no doubt catered particularly to Rudolf's

Mihály von Munkácsy, The Apotheosis of the Renaissance, with the assembly of the leading artists of the time before Pope Julius II. Rovere. Ceiling painting above the staircase.

predilection for erotic subjects. His picture gallery must have been considered a legacy carrying obligations, and a philosophical premise for later Habsburg collectors.

The actual founder of the Viennese Gallery was Archduke Leopold Wilhelm 1614–1662), brother of Emperor Ferdinand III. He acquired his pictures almost exclusively while governor of the Netherlands (1647–1656), a period which coincided with the Commonwealth's disposal of Charles I's collection in England and the confiscation and auctioning of various British aristocratic collections. The pictures were subsequently shared out; Leopold Wilhelm set up a collection of about 1,400 pictures of his own, and bought paintings for Prague on behalf of his imperial brother, to replace those looted by the Swedes. The archduke's own collection (mainly Venetian and northern Italian painting of the fifteenth and sixteenth centuries and Flemish painting of the fifteenth to seventeenth centuries) was moved to Vienna in 1656, installed in the Stallburg (the imperial stables), catalogued in exemplary fashion, and in 1662 passed into the hands of Empero Leopold I.

In the 1720s, a large proportion of Ferdinand III's collection in Prague wa likewise transferred to Vienna during the reorganisation of the imperial art collec tions under Charles VI. They were exhibited with Leopold Wilhelm's collection together with the many pictures that had been initially documented when Charles VI reorganised the Stallburg and refurbished it according to Baroque prin ciples of interior design. The installation was imposing – its appearance is known to us from an illustrated inventory of the collection – but must have palled in the 1770s as a "frozen" and static affair, incapable of expansion. There was pressure for change especially in the late 1770s and 1780s during the reign of Maria Theresia and Joseph II, when there was a significant amassing of mainly large-format Flemish and Italian altarpieces from dissolved monasteries and churches. This aug mented the collection considerably.

In 1776 Maria Theresia decided that the imperial art gallery in the Upper Belve dere palace should be open to the public. By 1781, the work of rehanging the collection along historical lines had been completed. Arrangement and the first printed catalogue reflect the spirit of the Enlightenment in the system they adopted and in the emphasis on education.

Napoleon's conquest of Vienna in 1809 was a disaster, involving a considerable loss of pictures. Worse still, during the nineteenth century, when the great na tional galleries in Germany and England were flourishing, there was an almost total stop in acquisitions in the imperial collections. The main thrust of activity - and then only in the last quarter of the century – was the total internal and ex ternal reorganisation of the entire imperial art collections and their unification in a new, purpose-built museum – the *Kunsthistorisches Museum* –, where the paint ings occupy the principal floor.

Collecting only resumed in the first half of the twentieth century, particularly during Gustav Glück's time as director, though under extremely arduous eco nomic conditions. However, even then the aim was to reinforce traditional fields of collecting and fill gaps in the periods and regions that had given the painting collection its best pictures, rather than conquer new territories.

ST. SEBASTIAN

Andrea Mantegna
(Isola di Cartura 1430/31 –
1506 Mantua)
C. 1457/59
Wood, height 68 cm,
width 30 cm
Inv. No. GG 301

Mantegna was one of the leading figures of the northern Italian early Renaissance and played a critical part in its development, both theoretically and practically. He saw classical art as a model for the realistic representation of bodies and perpective. The nude figure of the Roman martyr St. Sebastian thus looks almost like a stone sculpture. Thanks to the clear modelling, the three-dimensional physicality can be convincingly perceived, while the scene in the background extends artfully away into the far distance, punctuated by fragments of classical architecture. Mantegna wrote his signature in Greek characters on the pier of the triumphal arch, as additional proof of his familiarity with the world of antiquity.

THE MADONNA AND CHILD WITH SS NICHOLAS OF BARI, ANASTASIA, URSULA AND DOMINIC (SACRA CONVERSAZIONE)

Antonello da Messina
(Messina c. 1430–1479 Messina)
C. 1475/76
Wood, height 115 cm, width 133 cm
Inv. No. GG 2574

In Naples, Antonello had come into contact with the court of the Anjou kings and Franco-Flemish art, learning thereby the technique of oil painting, which was then unknown in Italy. The altar painting that he executed for the church of S. Cassiano in Venice in 1475/76 thus introduced oil painting as an alternative to tempera to northern Italy as well. What survives today is only a fragment. It was originally a high rectangular panel, showing eight full-length figures left and right of the Madonna in a *sacra conversazione* set in a church interior. In the new technique, modelling with light and shadow softens the hardness of sculptural shapes, and the subtle application of colour gives an idea of the materiality of things. The *Pala of S. Cassiano* was much admired by Antonello's contemporaries, and had a lasting influence on the development of Venetian painting, from Bellini to Titian.

THE BAPTISM OF CHRIST
Pietro Vannucci, called Perugino
(Città della Pieve/Perugia c. 1450 – 1523 Fontignano/Perugia)
C. 1500
Wood, height 30 cm, width 23.3 cm
Inv. No. GG 139

These days, Perugino's style seems the quintessence of an alien, insipid 'Nazarene' religiosity. Its representatives are sexless beings with a strong family resemblance, moving with distinguished delicacy, devoid of emotion and therefore in isolation, through expansive, light-filled landscapes or in front of airy architectural backdrops. This negative assessment applies principally to the works of the last twenty years of his career, when the quest for simplification of composition in the form of horizontal alignment and symmetry degenerated into pure schematics.

However, this *Baptism* belongs to Perugino's best period, and adopts a clever compositional idea borrowed from the crowded fresco scene in the Sistine Chapel in Rome dating from around 1482. In 1500 or thereabouts, Raphael joined Perugino's workshop. How much he owed to Perugino, particularly the Umbrian landscapes, and yet how wide the gap between the two painters is can be judged from a comparison with Raphael's *Madonna of the Meadow,* painted about five years later.

THE MADONNA OF THE MEADOW
Raphael
(Urbino 1483 –1520 Rome)
1505 or 1506
Wood, height 113 cm, width 88.5 cm
Inv. No. GG 175

Within the short period (twenty years or so, at most) we call the High Renaissance, Raphael's *Madonna of the Meadow* represents a classic example of compositions based on strictly geometrical shapes, i.e. equilateral triangles or pyramids. Within this apparently rigid geometry, there is room for plenty of lively presentation to offset the severity while allowing the geometry to set up parallels and contrapuntal motifs everywhere. Even the expansive green landscape, shading to the blue of the softly undulating hills in the background, contributes to harmonising all the elements in the picture by the use of related formal features. The figured group is thus simultaneously well-ordered and lively, a new and unusual combination of contrasting qualities, where nothing seems imposed from outside. This was a time when Raphael was also much influenced by Leonardo, who was thirty years his senior, continuing Leonardo's formal experiments with the Madonna format, a principal concern being to fuse motifs of spiritual and physical movement organically as reactions and counter-reactions, which would produce a vivid blending of formal and thematic aspects.

In Burckhardt's words, "it is only the purest beauty of the woman and the child that awakens the idea of the transcendental. After a millennium and a half, art was once again at a point

where its figures featured in themselves
s something eternal and divine, without
he need for any kind of extras."

UPITER AND IO

Antonio Allegri, called Correggio
(Correggio 1489/94–1534 Correggio)
c. 1530
Canvas, height 163.5 cm, width 74 cm
Inv. No. GG 274

HE ABDUCTION OF GANYMEDE

Antonio Allegri, called Correggio
(Correggio 1489/94–1534 Correggio)
c. 1530
Canvas, height 163.5 cm, width 70.5 cm
Inv. No. GG 276

Inspired by a work of classical literature,
Ovid's *Metamorphoses*, Correggio painted the amorous adventures of Jupiter
for a small chamber at the ducal palace
in Mantua. Among the canvases was
the picture of the beautiful nymph Io,
shown swooning in the embrace of the
god. Jupiter's face and hand gleam
almost invisibly through the veil of grey
mist he has conjured up to stop the
bashful girl bolting. Soft colour tones,
mellow light and light shadows blend
imperceptibly, playing on and modelling
the sensually yielding female body and
giving the cloud presence. In the figure
of Io, the emotionalised sensualisation
of surrender and delight, Correggio created not only a nude of unsurpassed
charm and subtle eroticism but also

condensed the profound substance of the myth, the union of living and inorganic nature, into poetry of rare magic. The picture of the shepherd boy Ganymede, whom the father of the gods carries off to Olympus in the shape of an eagle, was intended for the same room as the Io picture. Adroitly exploiting the (probably pre-specified) narrow picture format, Correggio evokes the impression of weightless floating in the free, air-filled space with a bravura display of movement and foreshortening. This kind of sensualised suggestiveness was a foretaste of the illusionism of Baroque painting, of which he was a forerunner.

an angel" (as his physical merits were lauded), and highly talented. He depicts himself in a fashionable fur, and exploits the distortions in a convex mirror he professes to be looking at so as to show his graceful hand, which "was so good at painting and drawing", to best advantage. Parmigianino's clever face lies at the centre of the curved reflections – he's proud of his brilliant idea, and he looks at us disparagingly.
Just to complete the mirror-or-picture game of confusion, he painted not on a flat panel but on a piece of wood that was appropriately curved. The purpose of the masterpiece was to acquire commissions from Pope Clement VII.

SELF-PORTRAIT IN A CONVEX MIRROR

Francesco Mazzola,
called Parmigianino
(Parma 1503 – 1540 Casalmaggiore)
C. 1523/24
Wooden tondo, diameter 24.4 cm
Inv. No. GG 286

PORTRAIT OF A MAN (CONDOTTIERE MALATESTA BAGLIONE?)

Francesco Mazzola,
called Parmigianino
(Parma 1503 – 1540 Casalmaggiore)
C. 1525/30
Wood, height 117 cm, width 98 cm
Inv. No. GG 277

This portrait of an imposing man is among the most impressive portraits of early Mannerism. The sitter with the small head shown menacingly close-up was possibly a famous Florentine *condottiere* (conceivably Malatesta Baglione), with the halberds on each side of him being attributes of his military profession. He owes his magnificence in this portrait not to the idea of perfection or the harmony between man and his surroundings but to the visual appeal of tension and ambivalence. The painter combines dissonant spatial impressions, incompatible factors such as sensual materiality and repelling coldness, physical presence and melancholy sombreness in a sharply defined formal entity in which discrepancy and unpredictability find expression.

As his name states, the painter of this small tondo portrait came from the city of Parma in Emilia. His self-portrait is among the most famous and strangest paintings of early Mannerism. When he painted it, he was just 21, "beautiful as

CUPID CARVING A BOW

**Francesco Mazzola,
called Parmigianino**
(Parma 1503 – 1540 Casalmaggiore)
c. 1533/34
Wood, height 135 cm, width 65.3 cm
Inv. No. GG 275

More overtly and explicitly than in any other of his works, Parmigiano here makes eroticism and frivolity the subject of his painting. Life-size and within reach, provocative and yet with an innocently covert backward glance, Cupid carves himself a new bow. He uses books as a workbench, seeming thereby to triumph over their scholarly content. Between his legs we can see two putti up to some mischief or other, although the little girl shrinks back from touching Cupid, fearful of being inflamed by passion herself. With its marriage of coded content and overt suggestiveness, the picture aims for sophisticated charm and effect. In that respect it is the quintessential collector's piece of the time. Parmigiano knew his elite market and exactly how to appeal to it.

YOUNG WOMAN AT HER TOILETTE

Giovanni Bellini
(Venice *c.* 1433 – 1516 Venice)
1515
Wood, height 62 cm, width 79 cm
Inv. No. GG 97

This painting of Bellini is one of his few late works on a profane subject. The choice of a nude as a subject is in itself unusual, and more typical of the tastes of the next generation of painters, particularly his two great pupils Giorgione and Titian. Here, Bellini's principal interest was a typically Venetian one – an endeavour to create an overall atmosphere that united interior and exterior, humans and landscapes through the medium of colour. In this regard, the landscape area manifests muted tones of all the colours that feature in the principal motif and recur in the carpet pattern as well. Almost all Bellini's pupils adopted the greenish gold background tone of his late pictures, which thus became a characteristic feature of six-teenth-century Venetian painting.

YOUNG WOMAN (LAURA)

Giorgio da Castelfranco,
called Giorgione
(Castelfranco Veneto *c.* 1477–1510 Venice)
1506
Canvas, height 41 cm, width 33.5 cm
Inv. No. GG 31

Giorgione's head and shoulders portrait of a young, half-dressed woman in a fur-lined mantle – possibly a courtesan – is one of the very few of his works to be fully authenticated and dated, thanks to an inscription on the back. The laurel bough *(lauro)* in the background could be interpreted as a coded reference to the name of the sitter or as a literary attribute. As laurels were also considered symbols of the (desired) fidelity and chastity in Venetian double portraits of lovers or married couples, it is conceivable that the picture is part of a pair, with the counterpart being a portrait of the 'Signor Giacomo' mentioned on the back. This work by Giorgione is a prototype of later courtesan pictures in Venetian painting (e.g. by Titian,

Palma and Bordone). The effect of the muted coloration typical of the artist, with fluid transitions between individual colour values, is enhanced by the sensual appeal of the soft fur on the light skin.

THE THREE PHILOSOPHERS
See page 142

Giorgio da Castelfranco, called Giorgione
(Castelfranco Veneto *c.* 1477–1510 Venice)
C. 1508/09
Canvas, height 123.8 cm, width 144.5 cm
Inv. No. GG 111

Although we have little documented information about Giorgione's life, the influence of his works on early sixteenth-century Venetian painting was of supreme importance. Born in the Veneto around 1477, he arrived in Venice before 1500 to learn his craft in the studio of Giovanni Bellini, like almost all the great artists of the time. He died of

the plague while in his early 30s. The gallery in Vienna possesses two of the few works that can be securely attributed to him, which can literally be counted on the fingers of both hands: *Laura* and the *Three Philosophers*. There has been constant speculation as to what this picture represents. One theory is that it depicts the Three Magi, another is that the figures represent the three monotheistic religions. More probably they represent the three Greek philosophers Thales, Pherekydes und Pythagoras. However, we are unlikely ever to know, because the subject matter is effectively private, specially tailored for an exclusively minded client and therefore deliberately enigmatic.

Nonetheless, an earlier title – documented already in 1525 – was *Three Philosophers in a Landscape [...] with those wonderfully painted rocks*, which highlights what was new and unusual about Giorgione's work at the time. The landscape was as pictorially important here as the human figure. Also innovative was the technique, which was geared mainly towards the effective use of colour. Using warm, delicately graded colours over relatively large areas, with fluid transitions between related tones, Giorgione achieved the illusion of a landscape topography filled with air and atmosphere. Instead of geometrically designed central perspectives, he used the optical experience of 'air perspective' or *sfumato*, which suggests spatial depth via blurred colours and outlines in the distance.

The novelty and intensity of Giorgione's expressive techniques – colour, light and atmosphere – appealed to almost all his Venetian contemporaries. Years after he died, 'Giorgionism' still held sway in the works of his successors.

THE BRAVO

Titian
(Pieve di Cadore c. 1488–1576 Venice)
c. 1520
Canvas, height 77 cm, width 66.5 cm
Inv. No. GG 64

This picture has always been celebrated, and it is not difficult to see why. It shows a sombrely dramatic assassination scene – a bravo was a hired murderer – and the element of mystery in the situation, where we know nothing about the background or the outcome. Taking advantage of a confined space, the moment of the attack by the assassin is compacted into the interplay of opposed heads and arms. In the confusing inter-meshing of gestures, we can identify the roles of the figures through the contrasts in colours – aggressive red and black represent the assailant, soft blue and green the surprised young man. Apart from the heightened tension in the subject matter, Titian's authorship is supported by the subtle characterisation evident in the painting style – violent and pastose with pronounced light effects in the killer in the foreground, fine and quasi breathed on as a Giorgionesque *sfumato* glaze in the background figure of the youth.

THE GYPSY MADONNA

Titian
(Pieve di Cadore *c.* 1488 –
1576 Venice)
C. 1510
Wood, height 65.8 cm,
width 83.5 cm
Inv. No. GG 95

This devotional picture is called 'Gypsy Madonna' because of her unusually dark complexion, and is one of Titian's earliest works. The harmonious unity of the composition; the balanced triangle of the group of figures; the choice of complementary groups of colours; and the dreamy atmosphere blending figure and landscape, foreground and background manifest a painter greatly under the influence of his teacher Bellini and his fellow pupil Giorgione. Yet even at this stage, the generous but nonetheless subtle wielding of the brush distinguished Titian from all his contemporaries. He modelled the volumes of things with the finest of colour gradations and lent them a surface brilliance that catches the eye.

YOUNG MAN IN FRONT OF A WHITE CURTAIN

Lorenzo Lotto
(Venice 1480 – 1556 Loreto)
C. 1508
Wood, height 42.3 cm, width 35.5 cm
Inv. No. GG 214

Lotto's early pictures reveal the influence of his teacher Bellini in the strict composition and clearly accentuated lighting. However, the meticulous realism of the surface testifies to the inspiration Lotto also found in northern European painting, especially Dürer, who had been in Venice 1505/06. Unlike the idealised portraits of his contemporaries in a High Renaissance vein, Lotto's portraits attempt to make psychic aspects visible as well. In order to bring out the personal qualities and the inner personality of the sitter, Lotto used a language of symbols accessible only to the sitter, which we can no longer really decipher. The little oil lamp revealed where the curtain is drawn back a little is one such symbol that was once an eloquent message.

HE VIRGIN AND CHILD WITH S CATHERINE AND JAMES HE GREAT (SACRA CONVERSAZIONE)

orenzo Lotto

/enice 1480–1556 Loreto)
. 1527/33
anvas, height 113.5 cm, width 152 cm
iv. No. GG 101

painter of the same generation as
iiorgione and Titian, Lotto started out
ke them in the Bellini tradition.
ut both personally and artistically he
/as a loner, and kept apart from the
fficial art trade in Venice in later times

Venetian art ever since Antonello's
Pala di S. Cassiano: a *sacra conversazione*,
with saints in an intimate grouping
around the Madonna. As in the portraits of his maturity, in this picture
Lotto broke up the hitherto prevailing
hieratic arrangement, prompted by
his innate preference for relaxed, more
human attitudes in the figures. The
Virgin no longer stands above the surrounding landscape and people as on
a throne but is integrated into the
group by means of glances, gestures
and posture. The close juxtaposition

s well, restlessly wandering back and
irth from his home city of Venice to
reviso, Bergamo and cities in Le Marche
Ancona, Recanati, Loreto). The art land-
capes of all these places contributed
› his work, so that overall it has little in
ommon with the classicism and idealism
f the High Renaissance, often tending
iwards pithily idiosyncratic, often un-
sual and out-of-the-way solutions in his
trongly subjectively accented outlook
n things.
¹ this devotional picture, Lotto opted for
genre that had been very popular in

and togetherness of figures and nature
is mysteriously enlivened by alternating
light and dark effects and filled with a
lyrically toned atmosphere that combines
divine and human, inner contemplation
and external movement into a richly
suggestive unity. The overall predomi-
nance of light tones in the coloration is
surprising in a Venetian-trained artist,
and probably derives from the colourism
of Bergamo, where Lotto spent more
than ten years.

GIRL IN FUR

Titian
(Pieve di Cadore c. 1488 – 1576 Venice)
C. 1535
Canvas, height 95 cm, width 63 cm
Inv. No. GG 89

The beautiful young woman that Titian recorded here with the coquettishly revealing fur mantle was his model several times, dressed and undressed, but always as a commission for the Duke of Urbino. The mature Titian's inclination towards monumentalisation led, even with such an intimate subject, to the use of large formats, which tended to give the sitter's face, bust and body a larger-than-life realism. As a portrait, it is a long way from the polychromatic style of his youthful works. The coloration is limited here to a handful of related tones, all shades of brown – from the ivory white of the pearls to the blackish brown of the mantle – in order to combine the variety of surfaces (skin, hair, fur and jewellery) into an artistically integrated unity of light and dark zones.

CCE HOMO

itian

Pieve di Cadore *c.* 1488–1576 Venice)
543
anvas, height 242 cm, width 361 cm
nv. No. GG 73

n the 1540s, the new design principles
f Mannerism developed by Michelangelo
nd his followers in Florence and Rome
vere also briefly adopted by Titian. Dat-
d 1543, this *Ecce Homo* was thus painted
uring the Venetian artist's Mannerist
nterlude. The asymmetrical composition,
vith the action running steeply from
ottom right to top left; the unexpected
isplacement of the normally central
ey figure to the extreme left edge; the
notifs of violent movement; and the
ashing, partly muted, partly aggressive
oloration are characteristic of Titan's
rief flirtation with Mannerism. The
ainting was intended for the Venetian
alazzo of the Flemish merchant Giovan-
i d'Anna (actually van Haanen) on the
rand Canal, which explains the choice
f subject, which was popular north of
ne Alps but unusual for Italy.
he picture shows the highly dramatic,
nomentous scene described in St. John's
ospel 19, 14–16, when, following

questioning and scourging, Pontius
Pilate, the Roman governor in Jerusalem,
presents Christ to the Jewish priests and
their followers with the fateful words
'Ecce homo!' (Behold the man), and
offers to set him free. The irate mob
demands crucifixion instead. The historical setting of the Roman imperial period
in which the Biblical events took place
offered Titian a welcome opportunity to
introduce a few anachronisms so as to
include the contemporary Habsburg
dynasty, whose ennobled court painter
he had been since 1533, into the picture.
Thus we have a double eagle on the
shield and beside it, as an annexe to the
signature, 'eques ces[aris]' – imperial
knight – as an indication of Titian's
esteem.

JACOPO STRADA (1515–1588)

Titian
(Pieve di Cadore c. 1488–1576 Venice)
C. 1567/68
Canvas, height 125 cm, width 95 cm
Inv. No. GG 81

Jacopo Strada was a universal Renaissance genius – painter, architect and goldsmith, numismatist, linguistic scholar, art collector and dealer and, by occupation, imperial *antiquarius* in the service of the Habsburgs. At the peak of his ambitious career he would not permit anyone to paint him but the portraitist of the emperor and the pope: Titian, with whom he also had business connections. The painter captures Strada's remarkable, many-sided talents in an extraordinarily dynamic picture that gives the impression of a snapshot, catching the subject as he goes about his professional activities. The picture has all the features of Titian's late style, when he began to use broad pastose brushstrokes to break up his previously more sculptural style with flecks of light and dark paint.

NYMPH AND SHEPHERD

Titian
(Pieve di Cadore c. 1488–1576 Venice)
C. 1570/75
Canvas, height 149.6 cm, width 187 cm
Inv. No. GG 1825

Among the few works of Titian's very last years is this *Nymph and Shepherd*. Despite the large, imposing format, the last of what he called his 'Poems' or 'Fantasies' was not a commissioned work. Titian painted it for himself, without having to take other people's requirements into account. It is not

nown whether he had a particular mythological subject such as Daphnis and Chloë in mind. More important than any specific narrative element as far as he was concerned was to depict human figures integrated into a mysterious-looking landscape – a theme he had tried his hand at in his early works when he was inspired by Giorgione. Sixty years later and with all the varied experience of a long career as a painter behind him, the task now looked quite different, of course. All that mattered was to show the scene rendered entirely through the medium of colour. Clear lines were omitted, as were the crisp contours and sculptural modelling of shapes on the smoothly closed surface, so that only here and there do occasional flecks of light shine out of the dark shimmer of the air, which Titian was the first to make 'tangible'. The visual impression gradually emerging from the weave of very broad, rough and at the same time subtle brushstrokes – he is said to have used his finger sometimes –

conveys in its totality the picture of a grandiose vision in which man and nature fuse into a cosmic unity. The huge range of painterly techniques in the handling of paint and brush that can be observed in Titian's work was aptly described by his contemporary Giorgio Vasari, the Florentine painter and artist biographer, despite his lack of sympathy for the Venetian: "The early [pictures] are executed with a fine touch and incredible care, so that you can look at them close up or from a distance. The last ones are daubed in rough patches, so that only from a distance do they […] appear finished." With the wisdom of age, Titian no longer rendered images of reality but approximations thereof in the form of mere visual sensations.

LORENZO SORANZO

Tintoretto
(Venice 1518–1594 Venice)
1553
Canvas, height 116 cm, width 100 cm
Inv. No. GG 308

In some of his most impressive portraits, Tintoretto moved radically away from the idealising approach aimed at formal representation favoured by the High Renaissance. He was interested in a more psychological, moral approach that involved depicting the individual, subjective characteristics of the sitter irrespective of his or her social rank.

The portrait of Venetian patrician and councillor Lorenzo Soranzo therefore contains no external tokens of rank and office; only his age (35) and initials are written on the parapet. The deliberately 'unofficial' casual attitude; the almost mystical glow of his face and hands in the intangible darkness; and the obvious emphasis on showing the spiritual side were designed to portray Soranzo the man, and how he stood out from the general social context which was normally omnipresent.

THE SCOURGING OF CHRIST

Tintoretto
(Venice 1518–1594 Venice)
C. 1585/90
Canvas, height 118.3 cm, width 106 cm
Inv. No. GG 6451

During the last years of his life, Tintoretto painted mainly dark, sombre scenes full of mystic expressivity. Coloration, corporeality and three-dimensionality are downgraded to the point of negation so that the figures gleam out of the uncertain darkness like schemata. A few broad brushstrokes of eerily flickering colour provide little more than a sug-

gestion of a presence – it is more like a picture of a vision than tangible reality. This Passion scene of the Scourging of Christ gains thereby an expressive quality of mysticism, which seemed to the ageing Tintoretto the only way to convey the mysteries of faith.

SUSANNAH AND THE ELDERS

Tintoretto
(Venice 1518–1594 Venice)
C. 1555/56
Canvas, height 146.6 cm, width 193.6 cm
Inv. No. GG 1530

Tintoretto's rendering of the Susannah theme can be considered one of the leading works of Venetian Mannerism, style that developed as a separate, local variant synthesizing the Roman and Florentine feeling for form with the Venetian painting tradition. As its founder and principal representative, Tintoretto employed mainly the technique of dramatically overemphasizing bodies, space, movement and light in order to overwhelm the viewer a sense of surprise and wonder. With the use of

of high tension inherent in the bathing scene is captured visually and concentrated in the sharp contrast between light and dark, extreme close-up and great distance (e.g. the view of Venice in the top left corner), the dazzling beauty of the woman and the caricature-like ugliness of the men, the assumed seclusion and the threat of danger. However, these formal fractures

Mannerist tricks such as exaggeration, distortion and the play of contrasts, a popular subject such as *Susannah and the Elders* acquired undertones of disconcerting provocativeness and menacing ambiguity that had never been there before but which really do constitute an aspect of the story. In the Old Testament we are told in Daniel 13 how, while bathing in her own garden, Susannah receives indecent proposals from two men who have secretly entered it. When she rejects them, they take their revenge by slandering her to her husband. Only the arbitration of the wise prophet Daniel saves her from the sentence of death imposed on her for her supposed adultery. The element

and contrasts are not introduced crudely and carelessly. They are artfully concealed with all the magic of Venetian artistry, particularly through the use of subtle greenish-brown tones and the emphasis on landscape and atmospheric elements, so as to keep the moment of 'calm before the storm' hanging in the balance. It is only with the second look at all the carefully positioned narrative and symbolic details in the scene that we notice the unexpected, indeed shocking connection between beauty and fear, whence this pictures draws its ambiguous expressiveness.

JUDITH WITH THE HEAD
OF HOLOFERNES

Veronese

(Verona 1528–1588 Venice)
C. 1582
Canvas, height 111 cm, width 100.5 cm
Inv. No. GG 34

Even a scene of such sombre content
as Judith with the decapitated head of
Holofernes gains an aura of decorative-
ness and festiveness in Veronese's treatment. The radiant coloration and stylish
beauty of the heroine allow us initially
to disregard the horrible deed which is
actually depicted. It is only at a second
glance that we notice the head of
Holofernes like an alien entity in Judith's
hands, more a thing of the dark surroundings than of her bright figure. But
this contrast between light and dark,
beauty and horror is what constitutes
the Mannerist appeal of the painting.
In the Old Testament, we are told how,
in order to save the Jewish people
from annihilation by the Assyrians,
Judith wins the trust of their general

Holofernes and cuts off his head while
he is asleep. With this trophy, she is then
able to force the army of the enemy to
take to its heels.

ADORATION OF THE MAGI

Francesco da Ponte,
called Francesco Bassano

(Bassano 1549–1592 Venice)
C. 1588/90
Canvas, height 304 cm, width 178 cm
Inv. No. GG 5801

As certain subjects painted by Jacopo
Bassano proved enduringly popular (the
Adoration was one such), they became
part of his workshop's standard range
and were painted again and again by
him and his sons, with various major and
minor amendments. This altar painting
by the eldest son Francesco is one such
free variant that uses individual figure
types developed by the father with their
typical diagonal attitudes but puts them
in a contemporary, rustic frame. The
wealth of what were considered realistic

everyday accessories lends the Biblical
scene a popular lifelike quality characteristic of the late sixteenth-century Bassano
workshop, anticipating the Baroque taste
for genre pictures.

THE SCULPTOR ALESSANDRO VITTORIA (1525–1608)

Giovanni Battista Moroni

(Albino/Bergamo 1520/24–1578 Bergamo)
1552
Canvas, height 87.5 cm, width 70 cm
Inv. No. GG 78

With his highly individual style of cool precision in depicting people, Moroni brought such quality and originality to northern Italian portrait painting that not only great contemporary portraitists such as Titian but even later artists such as Caravaggio and van Dyck were happy to learn from him. This portrait of Vittoria, the outstanding Venetian sculptor of the sixteenth century, is a portrait of a professional, a snapshot of the subject

as he goes about his daily business and at the same time a pithy formulation of what he was both as a man and an artist. Dressed in his working smock with rolled-up sleeves, Vittoria is seen with the torso of an ancient statue in his hands, as if to comment on his own work. Despite, or perhaps because of the sobriety of this representational gesture, which tallies with the sparing use of colour, Vittoria's figure acquires such captivating immediacy and powerful lifelikeness that for a moment we have the impression we are in the same room.

THE INFANTE DON CARLOS (1545–1568)

Alonso Sánchez Coello

(Alqueria Blanca/Valencia 1531/32–1588 Madrid)
1564
Canvas, height 186 cm, width 82.5 cm
Inv. No. GG 3235

Don Carlos was the eldest son of Philip II of Spain, and was severely disabled both physically and mentally. His character was unstable, and he was liable to violent outbreaks of rage, which caused conflict with his surroundings, particularly his father, who mistrusted his son's political plans. In 1568, he had him taken into custody, where Carlos died the same year from fever. Certainly the historical person was not compatible with the kind of heroic treatment that Schiller's play and subsequently Verdi's opera gave him. The portrait was intended as a promotional gift for the Viennese court. In 1564, there was talk of a marriage between Carlos and his cousin Anne, daughter of Maximilian II. The distancing required of courtly portraits is achieved by the neutral background, the physical rigidity of the figure and the sober, dry technique, which never allows us anywhere near the sitter as a real person.

ALLEGORY OF VANITAS

Antonio de Pereda
(Valladolid 1611–1678 Madrid)
c. 1634
Canvas, height 139.5 cm, width 174 cm
Inv. No. GG 771

The picture was painted when the young Pereda was commissioned by the court to join the élite of the Spanish painters in furnishing the Salon de Reinos at the Buen Retiro palace in Madrid with pictures of Spanish history. The *Allegory of Vanitas* seems also to have been a court commission, since the winged spirit holds a cameo with the portrait of Charles V in her left hand, while the right hand pointing at the globe alludes to the world dominance of the Casa de Austria. The antique medallion with the portrait of Augustus is intended to demonstrate the relationship with the Roman Empire and its latter-day continuance. The velvet-covered pedestal on the right with objects alluding to wealth, power and glory contrasts with the wide, bare table opposite, on which symbols of the transience of time, fortune, military glory, beauty and science are placed. "Nil omne" (all is vain), it says between the hourglass and the skull.

THE INFANTA MARGARITA TERESA (1651–1673) IN A PINK GOWN

Diego Rodriguez de Silva y Velázquez
(Seville 1599–1660 Madrid)
C. 1653/54
Canvas, height 128.5 cm, width 100 cm
Inv. No. GG 321

After Emperor Charles V divided up the Habsburg possessions he had inherited from his grandfather Maximilian I between himself and his brother Ferdinand I, the Casa de Austria split into a Spanish and an Austrian line. The Vienna Painting Collection owes the famous portraits of the Infantes by Spanish court painter Velázquez to the close dynastic links that nonetheless remained between the Madrid and Viennese courts, which were constantly being renewed by marriage. King Philip IV of Spain (1605–1665), the son of Philip III and Archduchess Margaret of Austria, was a widower who was also left without an heir after the death of his son Balthasar Carlos. In 1649 he therefore married again, taking his 14-year-old niece, the daughter of Ferdinand III, Archduchess Maria Anna of Austria (1635–1696), as his second wife. Maria Anna had been previously destined for his son Balthasar Carlos. The first child of this marriage was the Infanta Margarita Teresa, born in 1651, who was promised at a very young age to her cousin and uncle, the future emperor Leopold I (1640–1705). Until the wedding finally took place in 1666, the Madrid court sent portraits of the Infanta to Vienna at regular intervals, so that the Vienna collection possesses three portraits of the princess at different ages. The first portrait of the series shows the princess aged two or three in a pink gown. In this portrait, too, Velázquez formally followed the conventional style of court representational portrait inherited from the sixteenth century, where the key features were the sitter's pose and the setting (curtain, table). However, Velázquez offers us more than that, to great aesthetic effect. With the hand of a virtuoso and the free brushwork of his great sixteenth-century Venetian antecedents, he differentiates between broad swathes of colour and lightly applied dots of paint, to produce a picture of incomparable artistic richness and wealth of colour.

THE INFANTA MARGARITA TERESA (1651–1673) IN A BLUE GOWN

Diego Rodriguez de Silva y Velázquez
(Seville 1599–1660 Madrid)
1659
Canvas, height 127 cm, width 107 cm
Inv. No. GG 2130

A year before he died, Velázquez executed another portrait of the Infanta Margarita Teresa in a blue dress. By then she was eight. Cropped at the top, the composition is dominated by the powerful the silvery blue gown, which was typical of seventeenth-century Spanish fashion. The extraordinary width of this originally conical farthin-

THE INFANTE FELIPE PROSPERO (1657–1661)

Diego Rodriguez de Silva y Velázquez
(Seville 1599–1660 Madrid)
1659
Canvas, height 128.5 cm, width 99.5 cm
Inv. No. GG 319

In the same year as the portrait of the Infanta Margarita in a blue dress, Velázquez executed a portrait of the Infante Felipe Prospero. It was one of his last works, and was likewise immediately sent to the court in Vienna as a gift. It shows the two-year-old brother of the Infanta. As the sole heir to the throne, he carried the entire hope of

gale was achieved by the insertion of several strips of wire. The coloration and varying technique typical of the artist's late work, which only allows us to appreciate the rounded physicality of the model from a certain distance, are what make the picture memorable. The thin glaze-like application of paint in the head and hand areas becomes more vigorous and pastose on the splendid sleeves. The cool, metallic sheen of the robe forms a delicate contrast with the princess's flesh tones and the brownish background, which is only partially carried out.

the Spanish Habsburgs, but nevertheless died at an early age. In accordance with the traditional pose of courtly portraits, the child has one hand resting on the back of a red velvet child's chair on which a small dog lies curled up. The sickly prince wears a white pinafore with bells and 'protective' amulets dangling down in front over his red gown. Built up with a great variety of red and white tones, the portrait is an impressive testimony to the artist's virtuosity as a painter and his capacity for psychological empathy.

THE CROWNING WITH THORNS

Michelangelo Merisi, called Caravaggio

(Milan 1571–1610 Porto Ercole)
C. 1602/04
Canvas, height 127 cm, width 166 cm
Inv. No. GG 307

Thanks to a recently discovered document, the provenance of this picture from the collection of Caravaggio's patron and collector Vincenzo Giustiniani has been established beyond doubt, thereby confirming that the picture by Caravaggio mentioned by the sources as being in Giustiniani's collection is indeed the Viennese picture.

An important criterion for attribution, i.e. determining the chronological position within a well-documented oeuvre, appeared to throw up some contradictions. Suggested datings varied between 1599 and 1606/07, which were in line with earlier attributions to a Roman follower of Caravaggio or the mooted presumption that Caracciolo's – the most important of the Neapolitan Caravaggists – was the hand in question. However, a dating from the Roman period (1602/04) would seem to be the right one, particularly in view of the aftermath of this composition in Rome in the work of Bartolomeo Manfredi, Orazio Gentileschi and Dirck van Baburen. The comparatively open technique used in the heads, the summary treatment of the shoulders of the ruffians in the background and the slight underview tally well with the high position of the picture as a supraporte, which was how it was featured (so we are told – probably matching the original positioning) in the Giustiniani collection in 1638.

THE MADONNA OF THE ROSARY

Michelangelo Merisi, called Caravaggio

(Milan 1571–1610 Porto Ercole)
C. 1604/05
Canvas, height 364 cm, width 249 cm
Inv. No. GG 147

Caravaggio was a revolutionary both in his turbulent, violent personal life and in his painting. Deliberately breaking with the art of the preceding period, he achieved the kind of powerful effects on the viewer that the Counter-Reformation was looking for by giving the key figures in his paintings an overwhelming immediacy. Notable techniques he used were the dramatic contrast of light and dark (chiaroscuro), which gave figures and objects a theatrical brilliance and physical presence of hitherto unparalleled sharpness, and a style of rendering that rarely escaped into flights of idealisation. Though this realism may have seemed trivial to Caravaggio's numerous opponents, it was driven by the spirituality of a subtle artistic sense. The enthroned Madonna commands St. Dominic to hand out rosaries to the crowd thronging round him. It is not only the people shown in the picture who participate in the natural-supernatural event. Even the viewers who are likewise drawn into the proceedings by the gesture of St. Peter the Martyr on the right and the invitation of the donor on the left to put themselves under the protective mantle of St. Dominic and

ake part in what is happening. Whereas
he people in the picture only see the
aint, the faithful standing in front of the
icture experience the tangible work-
ngs of supernatural grace within their
arthly reality. Their attention is drawn
o Christ as the starting point of salva-
ion – the child stands exactly on the
entre axis of the picture – and the
Virgin and St. Dominic as intercessors.

The precise circumstances in which the
painting was commissioned, by whom,
and where it was intended to hang
remain unknown. It was probably painted in Rome, and around 1620 was given
to the Dominican church in Antwerp
by a group of artists including Rubens
and Jan Brueghel. It was bought for the
imperial art gallery in 1781.

THE CONQUEST OF JERUSALEM BY EMPEROR TITUS

Nicolas Poussin

(Les Andelys 1594–1665 Rome)
C. 1635/36
Canvas, height 148 cm, width 199 cm
Inv. No. GG 1556

The subject is taken from Jewish historian Flavius Josephus's *Jewish War*. Titus, son of the ruling Roman emperor, rides up on a white horse and is much moved by the sight of the Temple of Solomon being destroyed – against his wish, but in fulfilment of an Old Testament prophecy. The chaos of the dramatic subject is translated by Poussin into an orderly pictorial composition. In the rigour of the design and clarity of space, in which everything occupies its appropriate position, this picture testifies to Poussin's adoption of strict classicism, using relief-like compositions, sober coloration and a precise definition of bodies in space. The picture was commissioned by Francesco Barberini, nephew of Pope Urban VIII, who gave it to the imperial legate as the pope's gift to Emperor Ferdinand III. Was this a laudatory allusion to Ferdinand's victory over the Protestants at Nörd-lingen (1634) or a criticism of the conquest and plundering of Mantua by imperial troops in 1627?

ASTRAEA'S FAREWELL

Salvator Rosa

(Arenella/Naples 1615–1673 Rome)
C. 1665
Canvas, height 267.3 cm, width 169.5 cm
Inv. No. GG 9823

Painter and poet Salvator Rosa, a controversial figure who was both highly praised and condemned during his lifetime, is represented in the Vienna Picture Gallery not only by this picture but also by an early work that treats a related subject in a different way – the *Return of Astraea* (c. 1645, inv. no. GG 1613). Both works are political and moral allegories. The early one in the smaller format derives from the tradition of *bamboccianti*, i.e. it 'packages' the solemn proclamation of a new Golden Age (in this case the rule of the Medici) as a popular genre scene.

The other, late picture brings together the threads of the Astraea myth as handed down by Virgil, Ovid and their ommentators. During the Golden Age, he heavenly virgin Astraea lived on arth as the embodiment of justice, at a me when mankind was simple and ghteous. Later, at the beginning of the on Age, Astraea was the last deity to ave earth, repelled by the depravity nd cruelty of mankind. Instead, she ook her place in the firmament as the onstellation Virgo, together with her ttributes of scales and a lion. Before she ft earth, she lived among country folk, here "untroubled calm and life in honst simplicity" were not wanting, and ustice left her final traces with the easants before she vanished." he early picture, the *Return of Astraea*, ustrates the evocation of the new ugustan age in Virgil's Fourth Eclogue.

Rosa's aim to paint a second completely different version of the subject is already evident in a letter he wrote to his writer friend Ricciardi in 1651: "You remember that I wanted to do something different with just a few figures. And as it's an upright canvas, a figure could easily fit into the air, on a cloud or something. I've been thinking […] that maybe that story from Virgil's *Georgics* would be suitable – when Justice leaves the earth and hands her sword and scales to a few shepherds."

THE BAPTISM OF CHRIST

Guido Reni
(Bologna 1575–1642 Bologna)
C. 1622/23
Canvas, height 263.5 cm, width 186.5 cm
Inv. No. GG 222

St. John the Baptist preaches by the River Jordan, calling on the people of Israel to repent. Then he baptises and proclaims the coming of the Messiah. At the beginning of his public preaching, Jesus of Nazareth appears. When he enters the river to accept baptism humbly from St. John's hand, the Holy Spirit descends in the shape of a dove. The sky opens, and God's voice is heard "This is my beloved Son, in whom I am well pleased" (St. Matthew 3).

Reni abbreviates and concentrates what is traditionally a crowd scene, retaining only Jesus, St. John and three angels, who hold the clothes Jesus has discarded. Behind them is a landscape. A realistic treatment of an imagined reality –

t. John, the hermit who preaches in
he wilderness, is tanned from his outdoor life, compared with the light-
skinned, delicate, almost feminine-
looking future Redeemer – and idealised
figures and landscape, earthly and
divine elements fuse in a solemn scene,
whose balanced composition goes back
to the art of the High Renaissance,
Perugino and the early Raphael.

THE LUTE PLAYER

Bernardo Strozzi, called Il Capuccino

(Genoa 1581 – 1644 Venice)
C. 1640/44
Canvas, height 92 cm, width 76 cm
Inv. No. GG 1612

Strozzi was a Capuchin monk from
Genoa and later an unattached secular
priest in Venice. In his painting he was
eclectic, adopting numerous styles. In
this picture, he came up with a particularly poetic version of a subject that
was popular in early sixteenth-century
Venetian painting but also with Caravaggio and his followers. The lute player
listens attentively to his own tuning of
the lute, and yet he is above all reality,
inspired and getting in the mood. In
Strozzi's later work, his brushwork
becomes steadily freer, in some cases
extremely pastose and "spotty", but
sometimes full of fine shading and
rather fluffy, blurring outlines.

THE FALL OF THE REBEL ANGELS

Luca Giordano
(Naples 1634–1705 Naples)
C. 1665
Canvas, height 419 cm, width 283 cm
Inv. No. GG 350

The work of Luca Giordano stands out for its extraordinary range and unusual capacity to take very different stylistic approaches on board and adapt them to his own ends. Historically, he represents the end of High Baroque decorative art and the beginning of eighteenth-century Italian rococo art, particularly in his interest in the problems of colourism.

This painting is one of his earlier works, and was commissioned by the Bartolotti family for the Minorite church in Vienna. It is documented as being in the imperial collection since 1796. The desperate screams and distorted faces of the defeated angel devils owe much to the harsh verism of Ribera, and the sophisticated coloration of the St. Michael figure was likewise strongly influenced by the neo-Venetian palette of Ribera. At the same time, there is in the elegantly hovering figure of the archangel a touch of the classical antecedent of Guido Reni in S. Maria della Concezione in Rome.

THE DEPOSITION

Francesco Solimena
Canale di Serino/Avellino 1657–
1747 Barra/Naples)
c. 1730/31
Canvas, height 398 cm,
width 223 cm
Inv. No. GG 3507

Under Austrian rule in Naples (1707–1734), the city's leading artists worked for the Austrian aristocracy, the imperial court and Prince Eugene of Savoy. For the last-named, Solimena painted a *Resurrection of Christ* (which has remained in situ in the palace chapel at the Upper Belvedere in Vienna) and this *Deposition* (formerly in Schlosshof east of Vienna). It is clear why Solimena became one of the most influential painters for Central European Rococo art in particular, with a school of followers: he added a decorative structure based on a rich play of light and shadow and an assured hand-

ling of colour highlights to the heavy, sombrely expressive style of seventeenth-century Naples. In contrast to Luca Giordano's visionary, fantastic, open style, Solimena always maintained a strictly formal structure in his compositions despite all the extravagant movement, giving the figures sculptural solidity and moderated expressiveness.

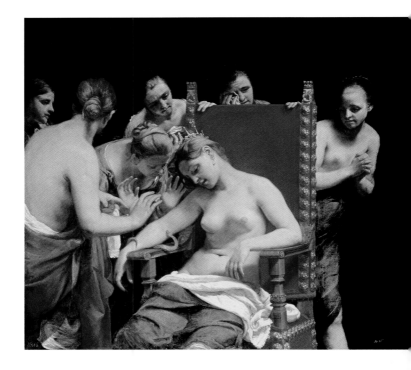

THE SUICIDE OF CLEOPATRA

Guido Cagnacci
(Sant' Arcangelo di Romagna 1601–1663
Vienna)
C. 1659/63
Canvas, height 140 cm, width 159.5 cm
Inv. No. GG 260

The last queen of Egypt, Cleopatra VII
(51–30 BC) killed herself with a poison-
ous snake in order to avoid the humilia-
tion of being led through Rome in Octavian's triumphal procession. Cagnacci
was court painter in Vienna, but had
never denied his training among Guido
Reni's followers; thanks to his visits to
Rome he was also familiar with the work
of Caravaggio and his successors, especially Orazio Gentileschi. In this masterpiece of Bolognese Baroque painting,
Cagnacci sought to combine the two
stylistic approaches. A sharply observant
realism in the expressive body language
of the weeping, distressed serving
women contrasts strangely with the classicism of the calmly relaxed Cleopatra

sitting between them. The figures are
bathed in a soft light reminiscent of
Correggio, where the tonal values run
into each other and confer an utterly
sensual character on the scene.

THE CENTAUR CHIRON TEACHES ACHILLES ARCHERY

Giuseppe Maria Crespi
(Bologna 1665–1747 Bologna)
C. 1695
Canvas, height 126 cm, width 124 cm
Inv. No. GG 270

Achilles was handed over by his mother
Thetis to the wise centaur Chiron to be
educated. This is why there are books
and equipment for astronomical instruction lying on the floor accompanying
the main action. The sources report
(partly critically) that Crespi wanted to
show Chiron punishing the young
Achilles for a bad shot by kicking him
with his hoof. Prince Eugene of Savoy
commissioned this painting from Crespi,
followed by four other Bolognese pic-

ures for his town palace in Vienna's
Himmelpfortgasse. In the mid-1720s, the
Achilles and its counterpart, Crespi's
Aeneas and the Sibyll, were being used
as supraportes in the Prince's State Bed.
Crespi represents a second highpoint in
the great tradition of Bolognese painting. Although he never threw off his
Bolognese artistic legacy and always
retained a clarity of compositional concept, in reworking the primarily graphic
structure of the picture in a more
painterly vein he marks the beginning
of a new era.

THE DEATH OF CONSUL LUCIUS JUNIUS BRUTUS

See page 168

Giovanni Battista Tiepolo
(Venice 1696 – 1770 Madrid)
C. 1728/30
Canvas, height 383 cm, width 182 cm
Inv. No. GG 6798

In the late 1720s, Tiepolo executed a
ten-part series of canvas pictures for the
main hall of the Palazzo Dolfin near
S. Pantalon in Venice, illustrating heroic
events from Livy's *History of Rome.* This
picture shows the death of Lucius Junius
Brutus, the first Roman consul. According
to Livy, Aruns, son of the last Etruscan
king of Rome Tarquinius Superbus, who
had been overthrown by the Romans,
attacked Lucius and in the following
hand-to-hand combat both men were
killed. When one recalls the desperate
political and military situation of Venice

in the eighteenth century, it may seem bordering on the ludicrous that the Venetian aristocracy of the time was boasting of the virtues of the Roman republic. Even so, the huge pictures by Tiepolo with their stormy, dramatic scenes and aggressive chiaroscuro, fluid coloration and powerful, solid-looking three-dimensionality must have made a tremendous impression.

EMPEROR JOSEPH II WITH GRAND DUKE PIETRO LEOPOLDO OF TUSCANY

Pompeo Batoni
(Lucca 1708–1787 Rome)
1769
Canvas, height 173 cm,
width 122 cm
Inv. No. GG 1628

It was the accepted thing for aristocrats on the Grand Tour to have their portraits painted by Pompeo Batoni. In this double portrait (in the original frame) Joseph II (1741–1790, emperor 1765), the eldest son of Maria Theresia, is shown with his brother Peter Leopold (1747–1792, Grand Duke of Tuscany 1765, emperor 1790). The picture was painted to mark the occasion of the brothers meeting in Rome. It reflects both the artist's classical view of portraits and the maxims of the Enlightenment, symbolised notably by Montesquieu's *L'Esprit des Lois* on the table. The simple composition is devoid of pomp and ostentation and yet takes the rank and dignity of the sitters into account, in accordance with their creed as enlightened monarchs. The Roman features in the setting allude to their status as educated monarchs who had been to Italy.

VIEW OF VIENNA FROM THE BELVEDERE PALACE

See page 170

Bernardo Bellotto, called Canaletto
(Venice 1722–1780 Warsaw)
C. 1759/60
Canvas, height 135 cm, width 213 cm
Inv. No. GG 1669

Vedutas – paintings and drawings with topographical reproductions of urban panoramas – developed in Venice as a variant of the landscape genre in parallel with the increasing number of travellers visiting Italy for educational reasons. One of the chief exponents of the genre was Bernardo Bellotto, the nephew and pupil of Antonio Canal, who like Bellotto was known as Canaletto. Bellotto was much in demand as a veduta specialist, working for the courts of Dresden, Vienna, Munich and Warsaw, expanding the genre far beyond Venetian scenes. This view of Vienna from the Belvedere is one of a series of thirteen scenes of Vienna

and imperial palaces commissioned from Canaletto by Maria Theresia in 1759/60. Standing on a prominence south of Vienna, the Upper Belvedere offers an extensive view across the city towards the Vienna Woods. The design of the perspective moves from the gardens of the Palais Schwarzenberg and the Belvedere in the foreground towards a series of grand Baroque town houses and churches in the middle ground – evidence of the rush of development in Vienna that followed the second siege by the Turks in 1683. Framed by the monumental domes of the Church of St. Charles Borromeo (left) and that of the Salesian convent (right), which structure the composition, we see the Schwarzenberg Garden Palace and Lower Belvedere with its Orangery. Behind the line of the glacis is the old city within the city walls, with the tower of St. Stephen's cathedral at its heart. With its roofs, towers and domes towering over the houses, the old town makes a very busy skyline. Despite the amazing topographical accuracy and precision, Bellotto took some major liberties with reality in order to achieve a harmonious unity in the compositional structure, for example reducing the distance between the two domed churches. The painting is particularly appealing in its striking perspectives, the fine, sophisticated style and the carefully chosen light situation: the warm light of sunset casts long shadows behind the avenues of trees and staffage figures, while the façades, roofs and houses gleam in varying zones of colour.

THE FREYUNG IN VIENNA: VIEW FROM THE SOUTH-EAST

Bernardo Bellotto, called Canaletto
(Venice 1722–1780 Warsaw)
C. 1759/60
Canvas, height 116 cm, width 152 cm
Inv. No. GG 1654

In selecting his views of the city centre, Canaletto opted for larger squares or streets with square-like open spaces, in each case dominated by a Baroque church or aristocratic palais.
These vedutas are generally smaller in format than those involving the major princely or royal palaces. The view of the market at the Freyung, which resembles a busy stage scene with genre-like decorative figures, is enclosed by the Scottish Church towards the back in the centre. Prominent among the aristocratic town houses at the back left are the Palais Harrach and Palais Kaunitz. Along with the light and dark contrasts

nd effective use of large areas of
hadow, the cold coloration with olive
reen provides the predominant backround tone which accounts for the
trength of the picture.

THE IMPERIAL SUMMER RESIDENCE OF SCHÖNBRUNN: COURTYARD SIDE

Bernardo Bellotto, called Canaletto
(Venice 1722–1780 Warsaw)
C. 1759/60
Canvas, height 135 cm, width 235 cm
Inv. No. GG 1666

This grand scene of Schönbrunn shows
the entire interior aspect of the palace
with the principal building, side pavil-
ions and the large court of honour. The
painting dates from after the conclusion

of the major rebuilding and extension works commissioned by Empress Maria Theresia for her summer residence. This scene was also accurately prepared as a drawing by Canaletto with the aid of a camera obscura, a simple pinhole camera. This is the only picture in the Viennese series which additionally records a specific historic event: on 16 August 1759, Maria Theresia waited on the balcony of the piano nobile for the arrival of Count Joseph Kinsky, bringing news of the victory of the combined Russo-Austrian armies over Frederick the Great near Kunersdorf in the Seven-Year War.

CARDINAL NICCOLÒ ALBERGATI (1357–1443)

Jan van Eyck
(Maaseyck c. 1390–1441 Bruges)
C. 1435
Wood, height 34.1 cm, width 27.3 cm
Inv. No. GG 975

Jan van Eyck is considered to be one of the founders and leading masters of Early Netherlandish panel painting. In 1431, Cardinal Niccolò Albergati, head of the Carthusian Order, travelled to the courts of England, France and Burgundy on a mission on behalf of the Pope in an attempt to begin peace negotiations with a view to ending the Hundred Years' War between England and France.

During the cardinal's visit, as Duke Philip the Good's court painter at the Burgundian court, van Eyck executed a silverpoint drawing (now in Dresden) from a portrait sitting, and he may have used this as a model for the oil painting. Despite the lifelike rendering of signs

of age based on precise observation of the old man's face, the portrait radiates dignity and calmness.

CRUCIFIXION TRIPTYCH

Rogier van der Weyden
Tournai 1399/1400–1464 Brussels)
around or shortly after 1440
Wood, centre picture: height 96 cm,
width 69 cm; wings: each height 101 cm,
width 35 cm
Inv. No. GG 901

Rogier van der Weyden – together with Jan van Eyck – was considered the greatest Netherlandish artist even during his own lifetime. He surpassed van Eyck, however, in his importance for the development of late Gothic panel painting in his wealth of invention and impressive handling of subject matter. The Crucifixion scene on this altarpiece is distributed across the three panels. The centre panel contains – along with the Crucified Christ – the main figures of the Virgin and St. John and their formal counterparts, the donors (who match them in size). The wings show St. Mary Magdalene and St. Veronica respectively. The background is continuous across the three panels, making it

into a single scene broken up by only relatively narrow, fake frames painted on the wings. Van der Weyden's style is full of pathos, with the intensity of feeling ranging from quiet sorrow to dramatic outbursts. The drama derives not just from the bodies racked with pain and grief but also from the deep furrows and broken folds of the robes blowing in the wind.

DIPTYCH: THE FALL OF MAN AND THE LAMENTATION

Hugo van der Goes
(Ghent c. 1440 – 1482 Rode Klooster
near Brussels)
C. 1470/75
Wood, height 32.3 cm, width 21.9 cm,
and height 34.4 cm, width 22.8 cm
Inv. Nos. GG 945, GG 5822

The diptych consists of two pictures
which appear at first glance not to
belong together. On the left is an open,
park-like landscape showing the *Fall
of Man*. The fine, miniature-quality

rendering of the trees and blooming
plants down to the individual leaves
gleaming in the bright sunshine is reminiscent of the sometimes overly precise
eye with which Jan van Eyck observed
his subjects. The first human couple –
seduced by the serpent in the shape of
a lizard with a woman's head – is reminiscent of van Eyck's nudes. But while
the left wing is wholly in the van Eyck
vein, the strong feeling of motion in all
the figures in the *Lamentation* on the
right is more like the expressive tradition
of the works of Rogier van der Weyden.

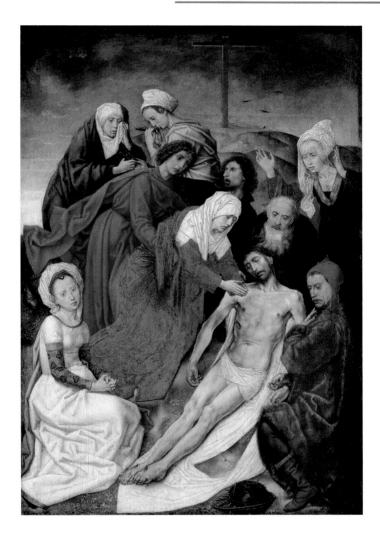

The angular stoop of the Virgin and St. John towards the body of Christ is echoed in the busy, broken folds of their garments. The bare hill of Golgotha forms a stark contrast to the bucolic landscape on the left, underlining the message of the diptych – the redemption of mankind from the Fall by the death of Christ on the Cross. This early work by van der Goes expresses eloquently the powerful tensions not only within the work but also in the painter's own life. His deep emotional disturbance ultimately led him to retreat to a monastery after failing to achieve his own unattainable artistic expectations. When the diptych is closed, the outside of the altar originally had a grisaille of St. Genevieve painted as a stone figure in a niche. The back has now been removed and is exhibited separately.

THE LEGEND OF THE RELICS OF ST. JOHN THE BAPTIST

Geertgen tot Sint Jans

(Leiden? 1460/65 – post-1490 Haarlem)
Post-1484
Wood, height 172 cm, width 139 cm
Inv. No. GG 993

This altarpiece by Geertgen, the most important Dutch painter during the fifteenth century, was painted for the high altar in the chapel of the Knights of St. John in Haarlem. The work was commissioned to celebrate the presentation of the relics of St. John to the Order at the behest of the Turkish Sultan. The winged altar was destroyed during the siege of Haarlem in 1573. What survived was one wing, originally painted on both sides but now sawn into separate paintings showing the *Lamentation* (likewise in the KHM) and the *Legend of the Relics of St. John the Baptist.*

A single landscape on the panel contains historically discrete scenes: in the background are the separate burials of the head and the body, in the foreground the exhumation and burning of the remains on the instructions of Emperor Julian the Apostate in 362, plus the discovery of unburnt relics and their delivery to the Knights' fortress in St. Jean d'Acre in the thirteenth century. Portraits of groups of late fifteenth-century Haarlem Hospitallers link the time zones and visual episodes. With this scene, Geertgen presents us with the first known example of the group portrait genre that later flourished particularly in seventeenth-century Dutch painting (Rembrandt, Hals).

THE BAPTISM OF CHRIST

Joachim Patinier

(Bouvignes 1475/85 – 1524 Antwerp)

c. 1521/24

Wood, height 59.7 cm, width 76.3 cm

Inv. No. GG 981

Visually, the religious scene in the foreground and the broad landscape carry equal weight. Although thematically the landscape is only justified as part of the baptism scene in the foreground, it is clearly the part that the artist really enjoyed painting, and the bizarre geological formation with the Jordan winding round it in the middle ground attracts the eye as much as the figures in the foreground. The rocky outcrop is the termination of a promontory extending from the left, which accommodates a secondary religious scene – John the Baptist preaching. As recorded in the Bible, a great number of listeners flocked to listen to him in the wilderness and to be baptised by him. The third section of the picture is the background, a 'universal landscape' extending to the distant mountains, with the prominent use of aerial perspective as all the colours merge into various tones of blue, thus creating a sense of distance.

THE HOLY FAMILY

Martin Schongauer

(Colmar c. 1450 – 1491 Breisach)

c. 1480

Wood, height 26 cm, width 17 cm

Inv. No. GG 843

Martin Schongauer became the best-known German artist before Dürer mainly for his engravings, which even his con-

temporaries admired and imitated for their rich formal inventiveness and technically precise execution. His small paintings, combining the strong draughtsmanship of prints with the brilliant colours of a style schooled on Early Netherlandish antecedents, appeal directly to the viewer's emotions. In his *Holy Family,* Schongauer conveys the impression of tranquil family happiness, lending the unprepossessing objects of ordinary life such as bundles of straw and grapes a deeper meaning in their allusion to the Christian story of salvation.

THE ADORATION OF THE TRINITY

Albrecht Dürer

(Nuremberg 1471–1528 Nuremberg)
1511
Wood, height 135 cm, width 123.4 cm
Inv. No. GG 838

In 1501, Nuremberg patrician Matthäus Landauer founded the "Zwölfbrüder-haus", an almshouse for twelve elderly indigent artisans. In 1508, he commissioned Dürer to paint an altar picture for the All Saints chapel he had endowed. Dürer was asked to show the community of saints with all Christians adoring the Holy Trinity, in accordance with St. Augustine's notion of the City of God after the Last Judgment. The Trinity in the middle – God the Father enthroned on a rainbow with Christ on the Cross and the dove of the Holy Spirit above – is surrounded by adoring figures in concentric circles. The innermost figures, and furthest from the viewer, are winged angels heads. They are followed by angels bearing the instruments of the Passion, then come the patriarchs, prophets and kings of the Old Testament on the right, with Moses (with the tablets of the law), King David (as a psalmist with the harp) and St. John the Baptist being particularly prominent. Corresponding to them on the left is a group of holy virgins and female martyrs. Notable among these (with attributes) are St. Barbara (chalice), St. Catherine (wheel and sword), St. Dorothy (basket of flowers) and St. Agnes (lamb). St. John and the Virgin constitute the traditional intercessors with Christ as judge. The lowest row is the community of Christians who have been judged at the Last Judgment, clearly separated into a clerical half on the left (the pope, a cardinal, a monk and a

**PORTRAIT OF A YOUNG
VENETIAN LADY**

Albrecht Dürer
(Nuremberg 1471–1528 Nuremberg)
1505
Wood, height 32,5 cm, width 24,5 cm
Inv. No. GG 6440

nun) and a secular one on the right
(emperor, king, princes, knights, citizens
and peasants with flails). Between the
cardinal and the mendicant monk is
Matthäus Landauer himself as founder,
wearing a fur-trimmed mantle. The
knight in the golden harness represents
Wilhelm Haller, Landauer's son-in-law.
Dürer includes himself in the extensive
landscape below, with an inscription
describing him confidently as the creator
of the picture. Dürer designed the picture and the frame depicting the Last
Judgment above (the frame exhibited
here is a modern copy of the original in
the Germanisches Nationalmuseum in
Nuremberg) as a complete entity in the
form of a modern Italian-style altar picture rather than the customary late-
Gothic winged altar. The style – an echo
of the Venetian manner – reflects this.

One of Dürer's key achievements in
the history of art was to progress from
German late-Gothic in the direction of
contemporary Italian painting. During
his second stay in Venice, he executed
this portrait of an unknown young
Venetian woman in 1505. It bears witness to Dürer's newly acquired ability
to dissolve the rigidity of shapes firmly
demarcated with line by means of light
effects that give brilliance to the
colours.

That offsets the sharpness of the outlines without destroying the graphic
clarity of the drawing. The young
woman wears early sixteenth-century
fashion with her blond hair – the glory
of Venetian women – in a snood with
tresses hanging down at the side.

THE MARTYRDOM OF THE TEN THOUSAND CHRISTIANS

Albrecht Dürer
(Nuremberg 1471–1528 Nuremberg)
1508
Canvas, height 99 cm, width 87 cm
Inv. No. GG 835

According to a legend from the High Middle Ages, the Roman emperors Hadrian and Antoninus sent an army led by Achatius on a campaign in Asia Minor. Although they were converted to Christianity by the appearance of helpful angels and subsequently achieved victory, King Shapur of Persia made martyrs of them on Mount Ararat, where they were crucified, stoned, chased through the wilderness and thrown over cliffs. Elector Frederick the Wise of Saxony commissioned the picture from Dürer in 1508, intending it for his great collection of relics in the abbey church in Wittenberg, which was exhibited once a year on All Saints Day (a practice banned some years later by Martin Luther). Two black-garbed men in the middle of the picture are conspicuous – Dürer himself, carrying a split staff with his signature on a notice, and his recently deceased friend, the humanist Konrad Celtes.

EMPEROR MAXIMILIAN I (1459–1519, PROCLAIMED EMPEROR 1508)

Albrecht Dürer
(Nuremberg 1471–1528 Nuremberg)
1519
Wood, height 74 cm, width 61.5 cm
Inv. No. GG 825

Maximilian I was the first Habsburg ruler to extend his possessions westwards beyond what is now Austria, by marrying Mary of Burgundy. He backed his expansionist plans with modern military techniques, but was shrewd enough to use the arts to justify his actions and ensure his posthumous fame. Among the many painters, sculptors and wood cutters who worked for Maximilian I, Dürer was one of the foremost. In 1518, he created a drawing of the emperor at the Augsburg Diet, later using it as a study for the first portrait of the emperor after his death. Maximilian is not wearing imperial regalia but is shown as a distinguished private person wearing a fur-trimmed mantle. Instead of an imperial orb he holds a pomegranate, a symbol of power and wealth.

CRUCIFIXION

Lucas Cranach the Elder

(Kronach 1472–1553 Weimar)
C. 1500/01
Wood, height 58.5 cm, width 45 cm
Inv. No. GG 6905

During the fifteenth century the Crucifixion scene with numerous peripheral
figures was among the most common
of commissions in late-Gothic painting.
In southern Germany in particular, more
and more bizarre or repulsive details
were introduced into the scene in order
to intensify the expressive force. In this
respect Lucas Cranach, newly arrived in

Vienna from Franconia, surpassed all
previous representations of the Crucifixion in this picture, the earliest of his
known works. Christ is covered in blood
and wounds; the Cross is a rough tree
trunk; the figures of the soldiers are distorted grotesques and ludicrously
dressed; the landscape with windswept
trees is rocky and desolate; and the entire
scene is painted brashly in loud colours.
This picture and others like it from the
same period made Cranach a founder
of the so called Danube School.

THE THREE AGES OF MAN AND DEATH

Hans Baldung, called Grien

(Schwäbisch Gmünd *c.* 1485 –
1545 Strasbourg)
C. 1509/10
Wood, height 48.2 cm, width 32.5 cm
Inv. No. GG 2636

Hans Baldung Grien was essentially a
pupil of Dürer, but he was also receptive
to the influences of the so called Danube
School, as this landscape with the lichen-
covered tree shows. It is a symbolic
scene of the various ages of man, with a
pronounced emphasis on their position
vis-à-vis omnipresent Death. The young
woman, her white nakedness contrasting
all too plainly with the half-decayed
figure of Death, gazes with satisfaction
at her blond hair in the mirror. Death
responds by holding up the hourglass
and clutching at her veil. Though she
ignores him, the old woman behind her
energetically attempts to ward him off,
to little effect. Meantime the small boy
with the hobby horse on the ground,
representing the first, immature age of
life, still sees the world darkly, as through
a veil.

JUDITH WITH THE HEAD OF HOLOFERNES

Lucas Cranach the Elder

(Kronach 1472 – 1553 Weimar)
C. 1530
Wood, height 87 cm, width 56 cm
Inv. No. GG 858

After Cranach was appointed court
painter by Elector Frederick the Wise in
Wittenberg in 1504, he soon abandoned
the Danube School style and adopted
an unmistakable approach of his own,
which was mannered in a style distinctive
from the Mannerism of the time. The
compositions are spatially flat, the settings indeterminate, and the palette was
strongly coloured and inclined to decorative effects. The limited repertoire of the
subject matter tended towards frequent
repetition, across various genres of picture. The half-length figure of the Old
Testament heroine Judith, who got the
amorous enemy general Holofernes
drunk in his tent and then killed him to
save her people, was painted in several
versions. It is Biblical history, a portrait of
an elegant lady at the Saxon court and
a costume picture rolled into one.

like a huge fire that lights them in shades of red and yellow and even reaches the dark clouds in the sky. All shapes are invested with light and colour, distorting them into bizarre figures in which the inanimate appears alive and the living seems petrified.

THE RESURRECTION OF CHRIST
Albrecht Altdorfer
(Regensburg *c.* 1482/85 –
1538 Regensburg)
1518
Wood, height 70 cm, width 37 cm
Inv. No. GG 6796

Altdorfer's large winged altar for the Abbey St. Florian, depicting the Passion and the legend of St. Sebastian, is one of the Danube School's most notable works. Two panels of the predella with the *Entombment* and the *Resurrection of Christ*, the last scenes of the Passion, are displayed in the *Kunsthistorisches Museum,* while the rest remained in St. Florian. The compositions of the two predella pictures are similar, showing views through the dark framing aperture of a rocky cave out on an open landscape. The *Resurrection* is a night scene. The resurrected Christ gives off a gleaming aura that illuminates the tomb attendants in their dull stupefaction,

THE NATIVITY
Albrecht Altdorfer
(Regensburg *c.* 1482/85 –
1538 Regensburg)
c. 1520
Wood, height 44 cm, width 36 cm
Inv. No. GG 2716

The Holy Family are grouped out in the open, with a scattering of new snow around them on the ground. It is night, and countless mysterious sources of light gleam out of the darkness. Music-making angels have taken up positions everywhere, each shedding a small circle of light. But radiantly shining on them all is the wonderful light of the newborn Child. It also lights up the huge ruin that towers above the Holy Family, a massive pier with the remnants of vaulting, and the buildings beyond. The supernatural nature of the light expresses in visual form the miraculous nature of the birth of Christ and the concept of Christ as the Light of the

World, as formulated in the writings of the mystics. The mixture of atmospheric and dramatic, of decay and rank nature, of the old and the excitingly new mark this little picture as a typical product of the Danube School.

JANE SEYMOUR, QUEEN OF ENGLAND (1513–1537)

Hans Holbein the Younger
(Augsburg 1497–1543 London)
1536
Wood, height 65.4 cm, width 40.7 cm
Inv. No. GG 881

From 1536, Holbein was court painter to Henry VIII. One of the first pictures he was commissioned to paint was of the new queen, Jane Seymour. Born in 1513, she came to court in 1530, serving her predecessors Catherine of Aragon and Anne Boleyn as lady in waiting. She became the King's third wife in 1536, immediately after the execution of Anne Boleyn. She died the following year after the birth of her son Edward. Holbein strives for the ideal royal portrait, rendering the costly materials of court dress with meticulous precision and old-fashioned flatness and rendering

the queen's facial features with cool objectivity, to emphasise the distance between the viewer and the subject.

THE DUISBURG MERCHANT DIRCK TYBIS

Hans Holbein the Younger
(Augsburg 1497–1543 London)
1533
Wood, height 47.7 cm, width 34.8 cm
Inv. No. GG 903

Holbein and Dürer were the only German painters of the sixteenth century to outgrow the closely circumscribed milieu of their native land. After training in his father's studio in Augsburg and working in Basle for some years, Holbein settled permanently in England in 1531. He was active mainly as a portrait painter. In his first years in London, his clients included a number of German merchants at the Steelyard, the Hanseatic mission in London. Even in small formats, Holbein's portrait style combines monumentality of form with an unwavering attention to accuracy of detail and painterly precision.

JOHN CHAMBERS

Hans Holbein the Younger
(Augsburg 1497–1543 London)
1543
Wood, height 58 cm, width 39.7 cm
Inv. No. GG 882

John Chambers (born 1470) was physician to Henry VIII, and this is one of the last portraits Holbein painted. The inscription in the background (added at a later date) wrongly states his age as 88. In fact he was 73 when he sat for a group portrait of Henry VIII's physicians and this individual portrait. The simplification of composition and monumentalisation is taken to extremes, so that the viewer focuses entirely on the unmistakable physiognomy, whose impressiveness is enhanced by the well-defined, mature expression of a man nearing the end of a long, rich life.

CHRISTOPH BAUMGARTNER

Christoph Amberger
(Augsburg *c.* 1505–1561/62 Augsburg)
1543
Wood, height 83 cm, width 62.5 cm
Inv. No. GG 889

No other German painter of the generation that came after Dürer managed to capture in portraits as well as Christoph Amberger the harmonious technique and calm assurance of the Venetian style. Of his extensive oeuvre, it is mainly the portraits that Emperor Charles V and city patricians commissioned from him that have survived. In 1543, he executed this portrait of Augsburg patrician Christoph Baumgartner on the occasion of his elevation to the nobility at the Diet. In the choice of the sitter's pose, the portrait succeeds in capturing the relaxed self-confidence of the man who has made it. Formally, the picture follows the northern portrait style with its view through a window to a distant landscape; nonetheless, the rich coloration and lively, open technique leave traditional antecedents far behind.

**MPEROR CHARLES V (1500–1558,
EIGNED 1519/1530–1556)**

kob Seisenegger
nz 1505–1567 Linz)
32
nvas, height 203.5 cm, width 123 cm
v. No. GG A 114

ith his full-length figures, Austrian
ainter Jakob Seisenegger, who was
urt painter to Ferdinand I from 1531,
tablished an international reputation
uring his lifetime and posthumous
me. Previously, head and shoulders
rtraits had been the norm.

Seisenegger's works, individual fea-
res were suppressed in favour of
verall grandeur of appearance, apart

from the essential physiognomical traits,
so that no external trappings of office
were required. Ferdinand I commissioned Seisenegger to execute this portrait of his elder brother the Emperor
in 1532 in Bologna, where Charles
had been crowned emperor two years
earlier. Titian did a now famous portrait
of the emperor (today in the Prado in
Madrid) which is very similar in composition. The question as to which of
the two works was the model for the
other, i.e. was the pioneer for a whole
genre of important court portraits, is
controversial, and still remains to be
resolved conclusively.

THE FIGHT BETWEEN CARNIVAL AND LENT

Pieter Bruegel the Elder

(Breda? *c.* 1526/30 – 1569 Brussels)
1559
Wood, height 118 cm, width 164.5 cm
Inv. No. GG 1016

The title of this picture relates to the main scene in the foreground, a tournament to resolve the perennial dispute between the carnival season and Lent. The scene is based on actual popular end-of-winter traditions going back to the late Middle Ages in which Prince Carnival fought Lady Lent with her retinue, particularly involving Shrove Tuesday processions of the carnival fraternities. Bruegel fills out the picture with other Flemish customs of the period between Epiphany and Easter, including improvised dramatics, masquerades and illustrations of church customs, to make a panorama of numerous mini-scenes, played out in the public arena of a market place bordered by an inn and the church. The chronological sequence is reflected in the topographical arrangement, so that viewers can immediately identify what is going on.

THE TOWER OF BABEL

Pieter Bruegel the Elder

(Breda? *c.* 1526/30 – 1569 Brussels)
1563
Wood, height 114 cm, width 155 cm
Inv. No. GG 1026

In the Book of Genesis, chapter 11, the Tower of Babel was erected in Babylon because the builders wished to "make [them] a name, lest [they] be scattered abroad upon the face of the whole earth." God punished the builders for their presumption by replaced the singl language with the Babylonian confusior of tongues so that no-one understood anyone else, and building work stopped In mediaeval exegeses of the story, the punishment is a result of human hubris. Bruegel reinforced the moralising message by a very presentation in his pictor design, reflecting sixteenth-century anti quarian interest in the monuments of th ancient past. The ruined state of such monuments suggested that, although ir the past structures could be large-scale, they were visibly incapable of completic The Tower therefore looks utterly solid. It is built on a broad base, and is shaped like a rock massif. Its huge dimensions

e emphasized by the dwarf-like houses
 the city surrounding it and the swarm
 little figures at work. When we look
oser, we can see not only the lack of
anning in the work – it is a jumble of
nished parts and unfinished parts still at
undation stage – but also the ultimate
nfeasibility of the structure.
uegel was inspired by the design con-
ept and shape of the Colosseum in
ome, which was deeply lodged in Chris-
an thought as the arena of numerous
hristian persecutions over the centuries
nd therefore a symbol of the hubris of
e past. However, what he shows is a
ructure that is actually projected
wards. Thus the ranks of barrel-vaulted
orridors all lead into the middle of the
ower and are therefore functionally
ointless. In addition, there is a second

secrets to us only gradually, because
we are misled by our empirical knowledge of rationally constructed Roman
antecedents. We are therefore initially
deceived into accepting it as a reason-
able design. Thus, over and beyond
its original importance as a symbol of
hubris, the Tower can be seen as a symbol of the failure of mere rationalism.

ontradiction in the design: the articula-
on of storeys of the radial corridors
ompetes with the rising spiral ramp of
e outer curve. All the verticals appear
 be related to the apparent horizontals
 the ramp, so that the whole tower is
psided. The building is intentionally
own as impracticable and therefore
capable of completion, but reveals its

THE GLOOMY DAY
(EARLY SPRING)

Pieter Bruegel the Elder

(Breda? *c.* 1526/30 – 1569 Brussels)
1565
Wood, height 118 cm, width 163 cm
Inv. No. GG 1837

The introductory picture of Bruegel's "Seasons" series shows nature in transition from winter to its re-awakening in early spring. As in the other pictures in the series, the view is from an elevated position at the edge of the village looking into the distance, showing an estuary on the plain below that has suffered all the natural catastrophes of late winter – storms, breached dykes and inundation. The typical seasonal peasant activities – collecting wood, cutting rushes, repairing house walls etc – are moved to the right edge of the picture, whence the eye is led back into the whole sequence of scenes. The children with paper crowns and waffles represent a carnival group typical of the popular customs of early spring.

THE RETURN OF THE HERD
(AUTUMN)

Pieter Bruegel the Elder

(Breda? *c.* 1526/30 – 1569 Brussels)
1565
Wood, height 117 cm, width 159 cm
Inv. No. GG 1018

The sequence of six "Seasons" series painted in 1565 – of which five survive, three of them in the *Kunsthistorisches Museum* – show the changes of the seasons and the outdoor peasant activities associated with them. They constitute not only a high point in Bruegel's oeuvre as a painter but also the end of a calendar landscape genre that goes back to late antiquity. The series divides the year not according to a rigid scheme of equal-sized periods (months or double-months); it shows each picture dominated by the idea of a season, although Bruegel originally started out with the older notion of separating the year into six periods.

Accordingly, the series, which we should imagine as originally forming a continuous frieze, begins with the old start of the year in March and *Early Spring (A Gloomy Day)*. The next picture in the series is the missing one. It was

ollowed by *Hay-Making (Early Summer)* nd the *Wheat Harvest (Late Summer)*. oth were once in the imperial gallery; ne was restituted by the National allery in Prague to the Lobkowitz mily, the other is in the Metropolitan Museum in New York. This picture epicting *The Return of the Herd (Autumn)* and the KHM's other picture, *unters in the Snow (Winter)*, complete ne group.

ach picture is a separate composition, ut fits into the context of the series, hich is organised by colour sequence. begins with brownish black *(Gloomy ay)*, continuing presumably via blue *Spring)*, then green *(Hay-Making)*, ellow *(Wheat Harvest)*, ochre *(Return f the Herd)* and white *(Hunters in the now)*. Two compositional elements ighlight the transitional nature of the utumn landscape: the returning herd oving from right to left (we normally ead left to right) and then in a diagonal towards the background and the llage; and the division of the picture to a left-hand section which is still in ne sun and a far right section dominated by clouds and a threatening storm.

The grape harvest going on in the background is no more than a supplementary detail, while the prevalence of places of execution with wheel and gallows reflect turbulent times.

THE HUNTERS IN THE SNOW (WINTER)

Pieter Bruegel the Elder
(Breda? *c.* 1526/30–1569 Brussels)
1565
Wood, height 117 cm, width 162 cm
Inv. No. GG 1838

This is the final (not the first) picture in Bruegel's "Seasons" series and is by far the best-known and popular composition in it because of its unforgettable formal inventiveness and dramatic colour effects. Shouldering their meagre spoils, the hunters are returning home to the village with a pack of dogs at their heels. They have turned their backs on us and the flight of trees in the foreground similarly leads the eye into the distance, as it were out of the series and towards the unapproachable, ice-covered mountains on the horizon. The actual 'labour of the month' in the traditional sense –

the pig slaughter typical of winter –
is treated as a secondary scene.
A pig is being singed outside the house
on the left whose sign indicates it is an
inn. Winter pastimes are also a secondary
element, featuring a throng of small figures on the frozen pond on the plain
below.

THE PEASANT WEDDING
Pieter Bruegel the Elder
(Breda? *c.* 1526/30 – 1569 Brussels)
C. 1568/69
Wood, height 114 cm, width 164 cm
Inv. No. GG 1027

This is the picture which above all others forged Bruegel's reputation as a
recorder of peasant life in Flanders and
reaped him the popular nickname
'Peasant Bruegel'. Forgoing for once the
elevated position that allows the artist
an overview, he appears to be right in
the room with a wedding scene in a
rich peasant's house.
The wedding feast is set out in the
threshing barn, the largest room in the
house, leading the eye diagonally into
the back of the picture, where the pile
of straw shows that the harvest has
been brought in. Above the bride in
the middle is the paper bridal crown.
Near her in a high chair is the notary
(there to draw up the marriage contract), and at the top the squire in
Spanish dress. The groom is not present, since he was traditionally re-united
with the bride only on the evening
of the wedding. Two bagpipers and

ervants bringing food and drink
front right, front left) give the scene
itality and naturalness that in no
espect lapses into comedy or carica-
ure. It is a frequent but false reading
f Bruegel's peasant genre to expect
ither of these qualities.

with the Habsburg double eagle. This
probably refers not so much to a particular ruler as to the power of the Habsburgs as a dynasty.

IRE

Giuseppe Arcimboldo
Milan 1527–1593 Milan)
566
Vood, height 66.5 cm, width 51 cm
nv. No. GG 1585

rom 1562 to 1587, Arcimboldo was
ourt painter to the emperors Maxim-
ian II and Rudolf II. In 1563 and 1566
e executed two series of allegorical
cenes of the seasons and elements in
he form of profile busts made up of
ymbolic objects. *Fire* consists of burning
ogs, candles, wick, fuse, oil lamp, flints
nd fire-iron, pistol and gun barrel.
long with the multiple significance of
re and the dependence of human
chievements on natural forces illustrat-
d, the picture also contains allusions to
he Habsburgs in the chain of the Order
f the Golden Fleece and a medallion

VICTORY OF KNOWLEDGE OVER IGNORANCE

Bartholomaeus Spranger

(Antwerp 1546–1611 Prague)
C. 1591
Canvas, height 163 cm, width 117 cm
Inv. No. GG 1133

Spranger trained as a painter in Antwerp and subsequently worked for several years in France, northern Italy and Rome. He was familiar with all the styles of his day, which appears to have particularly recommended him

as court painter to Emperor Rudolf II. The emperor had excellent artistic judgment, and took a personal interest in the work of his court artists, deciding for himself on matters of design and complex subject matter. The figures from classical mythology in this picture illustrate in allegorical form the abstract notion of the victory of knowledge over ignorance. As the warrior patron of the arts and science, Minerva places her foot triumphantly on the defeated and chained representative

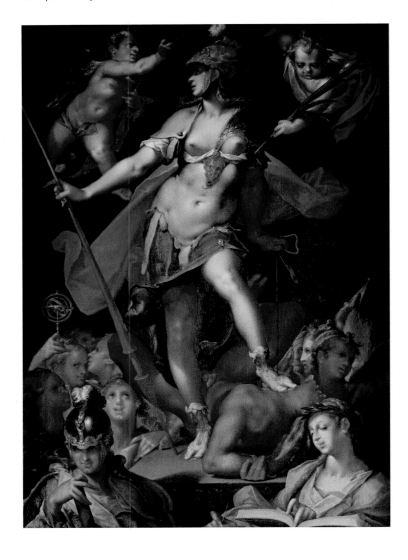

of ignorance, who has donkey's ears.
Surrounded by the muses and personification of the arts, the goddess demonstrates the power of the emperor's
virtues as a ruler in war and peace.

VENUS AND ADONIS

Bartholomaeus Spranger

(Antwerp 1546 – 1611 Prague)
C. 1597
Canvas, height 163 cm, width 104.3 cm
Inv. No. GG 2526

In his *Metamorphoses,* Ovid tells the
age-old story of the love between Venus
and Adonis, a young shepherd mortal
and huntsman. Filled with dreadful pre-
monition, Venus tries to stop her lover
going hunting for wild beasts, but in
vain. Adonis is attacked by a wild boar

and dies. In this large composition commissioned by Rudolf II, Spranger depicts Venus bidding farewell to her lover. Lit by supernatural light from the interior of the grotto, the goddess of love rests her left hand on Adonis's knee, turning so that the beauty of her divine body is fully revealed. The erotic charge of the subject matter thus matches the formal elegance of the composition, which corresponded exactly with the refined taste of the emperor.

EMPEROR RUDOLF II (1552–1612)

Hans von Aachen
(Cologne 1552–1615 Prague)
C. 1606/08
Canvas, height 60 cm, width 48 cm
Inv. No. GG 6438

Among the painters at Rudolf II's court, Hans von Aachen was the leading portraitist. He was virtually on terms of friendship with the emperor, and the familiarity gave him every opportunity to study the features and psyche of the emperor. This portrait therefore eschews idealisation and expresses the ambivalent character of the highly talented and cultured monarch. Rudolf's politics oscillated between determination and lethargy, which led to fraternal conflict with his less talented but more ambitious younger brother Matthias, who in 1608 largely deprived him of power. However, Rudolf's role as a patron of the sciences and the arts is incontestable. He made Prague the cultural heart of Central Europe by inviting scholars and artists to court. Equally important was his role as an art collector. Despite subsequent great losses during the Thirty Years' War, his Kunstkammer was one of the principal sources of the collection of the *Kunsthistorisches Museum*.

FLOWERS IN A WOODEN VESSEL

Jan Brueghel the Elder

(Brussels 1568–1625 Antwerp)
C. 1606/07
Wood, height 98 cm, width 73 cm
Inv. No. GG 570

Even in his own day, Jan Brueghel's greatest fame rested on his brilliant close-up flower still lifes, which were expensive rarities and much-coveted collector items both north and south of the Alps. Like a microcosm, they brought the beauty and variety of creation as reflected in the smallest objects into the secluded setting of the art cabinet. Brueghel composed flowers into huge, complex bouquets that happily combined artistic ingenuity and the miracle of nature in paradisiacal abundance. The flowers were both wild and domesticated, native and exotic, spring and summer-flowering, "as many rare and variegated as none before him painted with such zeal," in colours whose brilliance, in the artist's own words, "almost matched nature".

THE ANNUNCIATION

Peter Paul Rubens
(Siegen 1577–1640 Antwerp)
1609
Canvas, height 224 cm, width 200 cm
Inv. No. GG 685

Rubens completed this altar painting for the Congregation of Scholars run by the Jesuit College in Antwerp immediately after his return from his eight-year spell in Italy.

The Archangel Gabriel sweeps into the Virgin's cramped chamber like a whirl-wind. Mary's traditional gesture seems to indicate physical alarm rather than modest, incredulous rejection at the elemental invasion of the celestial into the mortal sphere.

Both figures react to the spiritual event with impassioned movement. The seduc-tive charm of the archangel with gold highlights in his hair and the warm, opulent iridescence in the 'Venetian' coloration of his robe contrast with the canonically simple blue and white of the Madonna.

THE ASSUMPTION OF THE VIRGIN

Peter Paul Rubens
(Siegen 1577–1640 Antwerp)
C. 1611/14
Wood, height 458 cm, width 297 cm
Inv. No. GG 518

Rubens painted at least twelve *Assump-tions* during his career. The one in Vienna is the first monumental altarpiece in the series. Originally intended for the high altar in Antwerp Cathedral (a pic-ture painted in the event only fifteen years later), this version remained from around 1621 to 1776 in the Lady Chapel of the Jesuit church there. During the lengthy genesis of the work, Rubens obviously changed the composition. The wall of figures (disciples and women) blocking the view in the background was split, opening up a view into the distance. In addition, the picture was cropped at the top in a semicircular shape. Stylistic features typical of the beginning of Rubens's second period in Antwerp (Herculean apostle figures and polychromatic coloration of the women's robes) sit alongside others (cool coloration, smooth flesh tones and tauter movements) more reminiscent of works from the middle of the decade. Overall, the picture is rather like the sum of aggregated details, and therefore looks static compared with somewhat later versions with their fluid dynamics and drama developing along the diagonal axis.

THE MIRACLES
OF ST. FRANCIS XAVIER

Peter Paul Rubens
(Siegen 1577–1640 Antwerp)
C. 1616/19
Canvas, height 535 cm, width 395 cm
Inv. No. GG 519

Before 1776 this monumental work alternated with the *Miracles of St. Ignatius Loyola* (now also in the *Kunsthistorisches Museum)* as the high altar picture in the Jesuit Church in Antwerp. Protected by the personification of Faith, St. Francis Xavier is shown as a missionary to Asia. He preaches to the heathen, awakens the dead, heals the lame and the blind, and has false idols overthrown. The catalogue of miracles of the two candidates for canonisation are synchronised (Francis Xavier was canonised only in 1622). Rubens executed a careful oil sketch (likewise in the *Kunsthistorisches Museum*) and prepara-tory drawings, but the actual altarpiece was largely done by his workshop. The artistic approach aimed at a clarification of

the theme (the content as well, if necessary), as well as an intensification of the facial expressions and an individualisation of the figures. Clusters of figures and overlaps were eliminated. Clarity was a significant aspect of the didactic and propagandist role that the Counter-Reformation allocated to pictures.

It was important that the message should come across clearly to the faithful viewing it from a distance in the vast church interior.

THE ILDEFONSO ALTAR

Peter Paul Rubens
(Siegen 1577–1640 Antwerp)
C. 1630/32
Wood, centre picture: height 352 cm,
width 236 cm; wings: each height 352 cm,
width 109 cm
Inv. No. GG 678

The *Ildefonso Altar* is the principal work of Rubens's later career, when he had cut the 'golden knot of ambition' (as he called it) and retired from his extensive public duties as a diplomat and political counsellor in order to devote himself

entirely to his art. This altar was commissioned by the Regent of the Netherlands, the Infanta Isabella Clara, for the church of the Ildefonso Fraternity in Brussels in memory of her late husband, Archduke Albert. As so often, Rubens turned to the popular winged altar format of the late Middle Ages. When closed, the outer sides of the altar displayed a view of the earthly idyll of the Holy Family sitting under an apple tree in the open air. When open, it shows a drama of solemn splendour in predominant tones of gold brown and red.

The eye moves from the representation of princely magnificence in the wings to the inner part of the triptych and the sacred realm of miracles and visions. Protected by their patron saint, the archducal couple kneel in prayer, as it were witnesses to the heavenly occurrences. In the dim half-light of a church, the Virgin has appeared to St. Ildefonso. Surrounded by saintly young women, she presents the devout figure with an opulent chasuble, which he presses to his lips full of fervour and humility. In the shimmering atmosphere and

vibrancy of colour and material, the busy but fluid, sensuous and yet shape-dissolving technique alternating between compactness and transparency, Rubens achieved a freedom and brilliance he had never previously matched. He thereby created a synthesis of apparently incompatible styles – the illusionist colourism of the Venetians he had admired all his life and the enamel-like, close-up beauty of body and surfaces found in Early Netherlandish painters – the legacy of his Flemish homeland. A masterpiece of painting of any period, the *Ildefonso Altar* seems both earthly and celestial at the same time, close-up and transcendental, a vision of colour and light in which the glorification of royal Catholic patronage is fused with spiritualisation and contemplative tranquillity.

STORMY LANDSCAPE WITH PHILEMON AND BAUCIS

Peter Paul Rubens
(Siegen 1577–1640 Antwerp)
C. 1620/25
Wood, height 146 cm, width 208.5 cm
Inv. No. GG 690

Two concepts for depicting natural catastrophes taken from classical literature lie behind Rubens's *Stormy Landscape,* although the painter appears to have added the mythological element only at a second stage of the work, to justify the elemental events. The carelessly added boards attached on all four sides provide solid evidence of the expansion of the original concept.

In the *Metamorphoses* (VIII, 620ff), Ovid tells of the elderly couple Philemon and Baucis who, alone among mankind, had offered a hospitable reception to the gods Jupiter and Mercury when they were wandering about the earth incognito. When Jupiter causes heartless, depraved humanity to sink into the bog, Philemon and Baucis are spared and are allowed to choose for themselves a shared death: they are transformed into trees. Philemon and Baucis's hospitable reception of the ods and their fate both frequently ormed the subject of paintings, but the ood aspect and the plea for deliverance were explored only by Rubens. The idea f a Deluge – a motif only hinted at in he Philemon passage in the *Metamorhoses* – probably came from another assage in the *Metamorphoses* (I, 262ff): ubens had in mind this classic flood which only Deucalion and Pyrrha survive) as punishment of mankind when e conceived his own idea for an elemental natural catastrophe.

However, the real subject of the picture not the myth, which acts as staffage, ut nature itself in its primeval power – ature at the height of its activity, hown in the way it affects human life ost of all, as destruction. We witness

storm landscape, Rubens was to some extent following a Netherlandish tradition (an early example is Pieter Bruegel's *Gloomy Day,* also in the KHM).

It is a theme he returned to several times. Some stylistic aspects of the work, however, go back to Venetian painting, notably Titian, Tintoretto and Bassano, also Adam Elsheimer (whom Rubens admired enormously) and the Carraccis. Yet as always with Rubens, specific antecedents are not really evident. Any influences he took on board in his work were fully absorbed and transformed into work which was unmistakably his own.

n overloaded sky, cloudbursts, torrents, ghtning, desperate figures drowning r drowned. Only two parts of the landcape escape this general catastrophe: he sunlit, paradisiacal level in the backround top left, and the sunny, wooded romontory protected by the gods in he right middle ground. They act as nchors of solidity amid the swathe of lemental destruction along the diagoal from top right to bottom left.
tackling this variant of the universal andscape type, which we might call a

THE WORSHIP OF VENUS

Peter Paul Rubens
(Siegen 1577–1640 Antwerp)
C. 1636/37
Canvas, height 217 cm, width 350 cm
Inv. No. GG 684

The *Worship of Venus* highlights the broad humanistic cultural horizon of Rubens, and his capacity to transform with the power of his imagination a great variety of external literary and artistic sources and forge them into a wholly individual, complex entity.

The starting point here is a description of the *Gods of Love*, one of the paintings in the *Eikones* of Philostratos the Younger. This third-century 'catalogue' originally contained 65 rhetorical entries describing real paintings in an ancient Neapolitan picture collection. The *Gods of Love* featured a rocky grotto from which water flowed to the trees in an orchard. In it was a shrine of the goddess of love Aphrodite decorated by nymphs, while winged Cupids danced, picked apples, quarrelled and were reconciled again. Around 1518/19, Titian used the text of the *Eikones* for the tribute to Venus (now in the Prado in Madrid) which Duke Alfonso I of Ferrara commissioned for his Alabaster Room. Rubens made a copy of that picture (now in Stockholm), and then subsequently produced various versions expanding, altering and updating the classical theme of the power of love. The expansion is physically evident here in the additions to the canvas left, right and top. Rubens' version is at once more precise and more general than the source. It is no longer the unspecific description by Philostratos that is the source but a modern interpretation of the Roman festival of Venus of Verticordia. Rubens was clearly a keen antiquarian, as can be seen in the temple and the nymphaeum on the left and the tripod in front of the statue of Venus. Verticordia fell at the beginning of April, which was Venus's month. It was described by Ovid in the *Fasti* and by Vincenzo Cartari in the sixteenth century in the *Immagini degli Dei*. The women of Latium, including girls and brides, celebrated the festival by bringing to the shrine of Venus flowers and other gifts (e.g. their dolls, mirrors and combs) to ward off uncontrollable desires, cleaning the shrine and washing themselves ritually. This accounts for the water features of the architecture on the left of the Rubens picture. On the other side, the putti, nymphs, satyrs and fauns should be seen as hybrid creatures that, though generally belonging to the realm of Venus, are symbolic of instinctive desires of the kind Venus could not yet avert. In his last years, Rubens moved steadily closer to the style of Titian's late work, recognising the affinities in their painterly problems. Echoes of the late Titian can be found in the open brushstrokes and richly differentiated colour effects, blending the atmospheric brilliance of the tones in the evening sunlight and the busy scene in the foreground into a unity. But the strong sculptural values and the ecstatic, orgiastic intensity in re-experiencing a classical antiquity felt to be wholly present, came from Rubens himself.

HE FUR

eter Paul Rubens

Siegen 1577–1640 Antwerp)
. 1635/40
Vood, height 176 cm, width 83 cm
nv. No. GG 688

he title, *The Little Fur,* came from
Rubens himself. The picture is probably
he most intimate portrait he painted of
Helena Fourment, his much younger
second wife, whom he used as a model
n many of his late works. Reality and
mythological exaggeration, private and
public aspects fuse with rare subtlety.
The young woman is full of naturalness
nd appeal, caught as it were on the
vay to her bath, but at the same time
as her pose indicates) representing a
ype of figure familiar from classical
ntiquity, the Venus Pudica. Rubens
hose a moment of particular charm
between walking and pausing, seeing
nd being seen, revealing and conceal-
ng. The picture combines sensual
visualisation with the feeling of a
momentary snapshot, in a tribute to
he beauty of the artist's wife.

SELF-PORTRAIT

Peter Paul Rubens

(Siegen 1577–1640 Antwerp)
C. 1638/40
Canvas, height 109,5 cm, width 85 cm
Inv. No. GG 527

Adopting a haughty attitude and
duly furnished with the aristocratic
accessories of gloves, rapier and hat,
the ageing prince of painters poses as
a nobleman for the last of his rare
self-portraits. Rubens was knighted
by Charles I of England, and as a
long-standing diplomat and political
adviser to the Habsburg governor of
the Netherlands, Sir Peter Paul was fully
entitled to use aristocratic trappings
for his self-portrait. But however aloof
his attitude and grand the setting, his
disparaging glance betrays him as the
artist himself, studying himself in the
mirror.

SAMSON AND DELILAH

Sir Anthony van Dyck
(Antwerp 1599–1641 London)
C. 1628/30
Canvas, height 146 cm, width 254 cm
Inv. No. GG 512

The story of the Jewish hero Samson is told in the Old Testament (Judges 16, 4–22). Samson owed his superhuman strength to his long hair, so when his

THE VISION OF THE BLESSED HERMANN JOSEPH

Sir Anthony van Dyck
(Antwerp 1599–1641 London)
C. 1630
Canvas, height 160 cm, width 128 cm
Inv. No. GG 488

Van Dyck's altarpiece for the Jesuit Confraternity of Bachelors shares a vision with us, an event that called on the

mistress Delilah cut off his hair while he was asleep, she was deliberately betraying him to the enemy Philistines. Though Rubens was his main role model, van Dyck nonetheless adapts his teacher's composition to his own style. Instead of the heroic, aggressive struggle to escape, it is the discovery of deceit, the betrayed man's despondent farewell to the beloved traitress and Delilah's conflicting emotions towards the lover she has betrayed that move centre-stage. Compared with Rubens this sentimentalisation of the subject matter is all of a piece with the unstable, diffuse composition; the action runs parallel to the frame, and the canvas is filled with an irregular grid of components in the scene.

artist's unique talent for painting human figures in order to capture the dream on canvas. His subjects often find themselves in extreme psychological situations, and here the painter succeeds in striking a tone of delicacy, charm and spiritual assurance rarely found previously in Counter-Reformation art. The focal point of the composition is the physical contact between the hands of the Madonna and the Premonstratensian monk. Van Dyck manages to convey affection and devotedness with physical conviction. The two figures strain towards each other, and are so engrossed in each other in the composition that it would almost seem impossible to release them. The expressive areas that matter artistically – the hands, the eyes, the hair and outlines of the robes – are systematically moved to the 'surface' to the physical periphery.

ARLO EMANUELE D'ESTE, MARCHESE DI BORGOMANERO

Sir Anthony van Dyck

Antwerp 1599–1641 London)
c. 1634/35
Canvas, height 175 cm, width 95.5 cm
Inv. No. GG 484

The portrait was long considered to be of Prince Rupert of the Rhine, but is now identified as being the 'Savoy Prince' mentioned in an inventory of 1730, generally thought to be Carlo Emanuele d'Este, Marchese di Borgomanero (1622–1695). Van Dyck always had a sharp eye for the specifics of a particular age. Although the boy poses as an adult as convention required, and the standard accessories of the courtly portrait are introduced into the 'action', we nonetheless see a face rising from the broad collar in which childhood and the threshold of adulthood are reflected with all their contradictions. The figure itself looks unstable, but uses the traditional architectural setting for support. Movement and stillness, pose and action are so intermeshed

that we are presented with an image of haughty, effortless elegance that still colours our idea of the aristocracy even today.

ARCHDUKE LEOPOLD WILHELM (1614–1662) IN HIS GALLERY IN BRUSSELS

David Teniers the Younger
(Antwerp 1610–1690 Brussels)
C. 1651
Canvas, height 123 cm, width 163 cm
Inv. No. GG 739

Leopold Wilhelm, the most important Habsburg collector of paintings, acquired his gallery of around 1,400 paintings mainly while he was governor of the Netherlands (1647–1656). The times were favourable, since as a result of the Civil War in England and the execution of Charles I in 1649, the collections of the king and numerous British royalists came onto the market. Leopold Wilhelm is seen viewing his collection in the company of his gallery director Teniers and other members of his retinue. 'Gallery pictures' – a traditional type of painting in the Netherlands – with (probably invented) views of gallery interiors were sent to other princely collectors of the owner's acquaintance. The aim was to convey an impression of quantity, decorously arranged. The present picture was sent to Leopold Wilhelm's brother, the Emperor Ferdinand III, in Prague. Almost all the 51 Italian paintings in the picture (in many cases shown with changed dimensions) are now in the *Kunsthistorisches Museum*.

THE KING DRINKS

Jacob Jordaens
(Antwerp 1593–1678 Antwerp)
C. 1640/45
Canvas, height 242 cm, width 300 cm
Inv. No. GG 786

Of all the numerous Flemish painters who adopted the new style created by Rubens, Jordaens and van Dyck were the only two who managed to transcend it in order to create unmistakable styles of their own. Of course, for all their huge innate vitality, the pictures Jordaens painted would have been inconceivable without Rubens as a forerunner. But whereas in Rubens the sensuously intensified verve is always stylised and idealised in a classical sense, Jordaens goes down an alternative path (also indicated to some extent by Rubens) to depict a florid, often burlesque reality. His exuberant and

acy interpretation of the rough and ribald side of popular life made him the quintessential recorder of Flemish joie-de-vivre. Unlike Rubens, whose direct study of life was generally associated with religious or mythological contexts, Jordaens also painted genre pictures. *The King Drinks* is in the tradition of the lively scenes of inns, fairs and boisterous feasts common in Flanders since Bruegel's day. The Viennese version is the painter's fourth and last treatment of the popular subject. As was often the case in Rubens as well, Jordaens expanded while he was working what he had originally intended as a small painting into a rich, sweeping panorama of a folk custom at Epiphany. The finder of the bean baked into a cake becomes lord of the feast; the most beautiful woman becomes the queen; and the company at table forms the court. Little labels show what offices they have been appointed to. Jordaens depicts the rambunctious get-together with an exuberant brush. Drinking and bawling, old and young,

men and women bustle to enjoy themselves in a wealth of movement that seems to burst out of the picture. The goings-on in the foul atmosphere of the confined space seem immoderate and chaotic, yet the pandemonium and disarray are only apparent. The composition is balanced, indeed rigorous in its near-symmetry. Soft light flooding through the window bestows not only human warmth and intimacy on the densely crowded scene but also divides the rowdy company into groups. The moral of the scene is expressed in a Latin tag: 'No-one is more like a fool than a drunk.'

TITUS VAN RIJN, THE ARTIST'S SON, READING

Rembrandt Harmensz. van Rijn

(Leiden 1606–1669 Amsterdam)
C. 1656/57
Canvas, height 70.5 cm, width 64 cm
Inv. No. GG 410

Titus van Rijn (born 1641) was the fourth-born son of Rembrandt and his first wife Saskia. Rembrandt painted some ten pictures of his son, who was the only one of his children to reach adulthood. The portrait was painted at a time when the artist was beset by increasing financial worries, living in retirement in his Amsterdam house with Titus and Hendrickje Stoffels. This view of the young man, seen diagonally from the front sitting in a chair, first encounters the book in his hands. The momentariness of the scene is emphasised by the slightly parted lips. The broad, unifying brushstrokes and adroit lighting model his forehead, temple, nose and hands sculpturally, highlighting them while the upper body remains in shadow. Light is used as a means of intensifying expression and singling put the intimate moment showing the young man's preoccupation with reading.

LARGE SELF-PORTRAIT

Rembrandt Harmensz. van Rijn

(Leiden 1606–1669 Amsterdam)
1652
Canvas, height 112 cm, width 81.5 cm
Inv. No. GG 411

In the *Large Self-Portrait,* painted in the year when Rembrandt's business problems first surfaced, the artist faces us frontally. He has his arms on his hips, with his thumbs tucked into his belt. Unlike the portraits of earlier periods, where he portrayed himself generally in splendid clothes or dressed up, here he

wears a plain painting smock. The typical cool grey coloration and fussy brushwork of Rembrandt's early period have
moved on to a subtly graded brown
tonality and broad, pastose brushwork
that unifies shapes and scarcely distin-
guishes any more between clothes,
hands and background. Only the face
stands out, emphasised by the vigorous
modelling of the brushwork and the
use of light.

THE GREAT FOREST
See page 212
Jacob van Ruisdael
(Haarlem *c.* 1628/29 – 1682 Amsterdam)
C. 1655/60
Canvas, height 139 cm, width 180 cm
Inv. No. GG 426

Whereas Netherlandish landscapes of
the sixteenth century show an aggre-
gation of various visual natural phe-
nomena placed side by side, around
1600 the genre sought a greater homo-
geneity and simplification of composition. Thus the paintings of Gillis van
Coninxloo (1544–1607), a Flemish

émigré to Holland, feature isolated clumps of wood devoid of any kind of staffage. But whereas in Coninxloo's paintings mysterious, bizarre, highly detailed thickets appear in the foreground, in the works of Jacob van Ruisdael, half a century his junior, the forests are seen from a safe distance. They no longer consist of a multitude of individual trees but form a unity. The composition is simply and clearly organised, with light filtering between the trunks in the background so that we know there is open country beyond. Man is inconspicuous compared with the grandeur of nature. Only by looking closer do we discover mid-picture a traveller resting and a couple approaching the ford. All this explains why Ruisdael's pictures were particularly popular in the early nineteenth century, at the dawn of the Romantic age.

THE ARTIST'S STUDIO

Johannes Vermeer
(Delft 1632 – 1675 Delft)
C. 1665/66
Canvas, height 120 cm, width 100 cm
Inv. No. GG 9128

Vermeer turned the everyday Dutch genre picture into high art. In his pictures, there is complete unity between the picture content and the balanced structure, where no element can be changed without sorely disrupting the overall harmony of the composition. Thus he completely excluded the element of the accidental which had hitherto been a feature of genre painting. The people in his picture seem to have laid aside their activities for a moment of reflection. The complexity of their mood creates an intensely poetic feeling. As Vermeer used the camera obscura as a technical aid when painting, it was not the immediate three-dimensional phenomenon but a flat image that he used as a model, which no doubt goes some way towards

xplaining the still-life character of his ompositions.

With this scene of the painter in his tudio, Vermeer took the genre picture o a higher level. It is a richly symbolic llegory of art in a double sense. It vorks with the allegorical armoury of ·aroque art, and yet would fail to con- ince were it not also a wonderful piece f painting. We look out of a dark area ast a tied-back curtain into the lighter rea of the studio. With the oversize- ooking chair in the foreground, Ver- heer very deliberately creates a sense f depth as an expressive resource. he painter sits at his easel with his

back to us, richly dressed in an oddly old-fashioned style. His model poses as Clio, the Muse of History, as her attrib- utes of laurel wreath, trumpet and book announce. Vital clues in the interpreta- tion of the allegory are the still life on the table, the treatise on painting, the mask or sculptural model and sketch- book, and the large map of the seven- teen provinces of the Netherlands before partition on 1581 that hangs prominently on the back wall. Probably the allegory, in which illusion and reality intermesh, should be deciphered on several levels: the Muse of History inspires the painter and at the same

time proclaims the glory of the art of the once-united Netherlands, which she immortalises in the Book of History. The painting was auctioned along with Vermeer's estate (where it was already listed as *Painting*), and subsequently entered the imperial collection via the collections of Gottfried van Swieten and Count Czernin.

BEWARE OF LUXURY ("IN WEELDE SIET TOE")

Jan Steen
(Leiden *c.* 1626/36 – 1679 Leiden)
1663
Canvas, height 105 cm, width 145 cm
Inv. No. GG 791

Jan Steen was a humorist who, with his illustrations of moral truths, expanded Dutch genre pictures into lively narratives full of comic detail. In them, the didactic strand is fully integrated into the narrative and realistic element. In *Beware of Luxury*, he shows us a slovenly household. Once the housewife falls asleep at the table, havoc breaks out all around her, the miniature scenes obviously corresponding to well-known Dutch sayings and turns of speech. The moral is given in the inscription on the slate bottom right with the first part of a Dutch proverb: *In weelde siet toe […]* (In a life of luxury, beware […]), the completion being 'and fear the rod', i.e. the consequences and the punishment. The instruments of the latter, the rapier and walking stick, hang threateningly from the ceiling in a basket.

SUFFOLK LANDSCAPE

Thomas Gainsborough
(Sudbury 1727–1788 London)
C. 1750
Canvas, height 66 cm, width 95 cm
Inv. No. GG 6271

The landscapes the young Gainsborough painted around the middle of the century, mostly in his native Suffolk, reveal the influence of Dutch landscape art in the choice of subject matter (here, a cart track winding into the distance between sandy banks) and trees and clouds building up in the middle ground. However, the firmly structured compositions of the Baroque antecedents are given a makeover of Rococo movement and lightness that is matched by the loosely curving brushstrokes and soft, honey-toned coloration. Characteristic features are the irregularly distributed patches of light, the curving outlines of the track, pond, tree trunks and clouds, and the graceful staffage figures.

Coin Cabinet

III. on pages 216/217 and 218:
Room I of the Coin Cabinet.
Medals, Decorations, Portrait Collection
of Archduke Ferdinand of Tyrol.

Interest in old coins goes back a long way. Treasure troves containing coins of pre
cious metals provided rulers with a welcome source of gold and silver. The piece
were either melted down for their metal or found their way into the royal treas
ure chamber, which might later occasionally form the basis of an art cabinet. Old
coins were particularly appealing for dynastic or political reasons, providing evi
dence of ancestors and predecessors in office. Coin collections are thus among
the oldest of all museum-type institutions worldwide. That applies to the *Münz*
kabinett in Vienna as well, which was based on the Habsburg collection but wa
continually developed and extended with coins from later periods. Over the cen
turies the collection grew steadily, and now contains 700,000 items from three
millennia. It is one of the five largest and most important numismatic collection
in the world.

Interest in both Austrian coinage and coins of earlier periods is documented
from the period of Emperor Maximilian I (1459–1519). Under Ferdinand I (1503–
1564), an inventory was taken of the collection in *c.* 1547/50, and it still survives
In it, Leopold Heyperger, the emperor's chamberlain, listed almost exclusively
Roman coins. Archduke Ferdinand II (1529–1595), son of the Emperor and Prince

of Tyrol, was an enthusiastic art collector and had a coin collection. His coin cabinets still exist, some in the Coin Cabinet and some at Schloss Ambras. Emperor Rudolf II (1552–1612), who made his Residenz city Prague a centre of cultural life and was a major patron of the arts, likewise extended the holdings of the Habsburg coin collection and also proved an important promoter of numismatic art.

In the eighteenth century, the Coin Collection enjoyed the personal attention of Emperor Charles VI (1711–1740), who was very interested in numismatics and intervened in artistic and technical matters at the new mint to make improvements. He appointed Swedish-born Carl Gustav Heräus as Inspector of Antiquities, entrusting him with the reorganisation of the coin and medal cabinet. Heräus came up with numerous initiatives and even his own designs for medals to commemorate historic or dynastic occasions. A handwritten acquisitions ledger kept by Heräus is important documentation of historical development of the Coin Cabinet. The extent of Charles's personal interest in numismatics can be judged from his having a special book made to hold coins *(nummotheca),* a kind of Baroque coin album, so as to be able to carry a selection of his favourite coins with him on his travels.

Charles's brother-in-law Stephen of Lorraine (1708–1765) was likewise an important collector of modern coins. When he became Emperor Franz Stephan, it undoubtedly opened up for him important sources for acquiring rare pieces. He was lucky enough to find an excellent, self-taught but highly talented Champagne born curator in Valentin Jamerai Duval, who put his collection in order and expanded it. Franz Stephan's collection is catalogued in two large contemporary volumes. A daughter of Maria Theresia and Franz Stephan, Maria Anna, likewise took up numismatics, and wrote a work about the medals of her mother that was published anonymously. After the emperor's death, Maria Theresia had his collection merged with the Habsburg holdings. This more or less determined the long-term shape of the imperial Coin Cabinet, as it later became.

Thereafter it was always run by scholars and experts. A Jesuit priest, Joseph Hilarius Eckhel, was the first of them, appointed director of the Collection of Ancient Coins in 1774, under Duval's supervision. A scholar of international repute, he not only published the ancient coins in the imperial collection but also wrote a *Doctrina Nummorum Veterum* that became a standard modern work on ancient numismatics.

The insights of the historical sciences and addition of new areas of interest in the nineteenth century changed the scope of numismatics. Interest in the function of coins as a means of payment and thereby the history of money enlarged the horizon beyond purely descriptive numismatics, and this also expanded the collecting activity. The Coin Cabinet now contains not only coins and medals but also paper money and securities, commodity money, die marks, stamps, seals and seal stamps, coin scales and weights, orders, decorations and historic coin and medal punching dies. Thus the Coin Cabinet is a collecting point for documents that represent money in all its forms and functions, and this naturally covers artistic and technical aspects as well.

When the new museum building opened on the Ringstrasse in 1891, the imperial collections, which up to that point had been housed in a wide variety of places, were finally united in the *Kunsthistorisches Museum*. The Coin Cabinet (including the *Antikenkabinett*) was initially accommodated on the upper ground level, but in 1899 moved up to the second floor. Since 1 January 1900, the Coin Cabinet has been a separate collection from the Collection of Antiquities. Nowadays there are three rooms exhibiting around 2,000 items, i.e. only a tiny part of the collection. The exhibition is organised on the following basis:

Room 1 is devoted to medals from the early days around 1400 in Italy to the twentieth century. They are arranged according to territorial origin, stylistic periods and cultural historical themes. Austrian and European orders and decorations are also on display. Room II documents the development of coins and paper money, beginning with pre-monetary types of money and commodity articles via the invention of coins in the seventh century BC in the Lydian coast area down to the twentieth century. The presentation is organised by historical periods and countries and coin nominals (pennies, thalers, gold coins, fractions of thalers and smaller nominals). The techniques of minting are also explained. Room III is reserved for special exhibitions.

DECADRACHM

*Master engraver:
Euainetos*

Sicily, Syracuse, *c.* 420 BC
Silver, 43.11 g, diameter 36
mm
Inv. No. MK 6.807

In Syracuse the art of minting reached
a peak in the late fifth century BC with
master engravers Cimon and Euainetos.
Both artists made commemorative coins
to a value of 10 drachms. The obverse of
this decadrachm shows the head of the
nymph Arethusa. She has a garland of
corn in her hair and precious jewellery

on her neck and ears. Her head is surrounded by dolphins, symbolising the
sea. On the reverse is the victorious
driver of a quadriga, crowned by Nike
flying overhead. The exergue shows
the victor's prize – a complete set of
warrior's armour.

TETRADRACHM

Macedonia, Alexander the Great
Silver, 16.86 g, diameter 28 mm
Inv. No. MK 35.760

Following his conquests, Alexander III
the Great (336–323) was able to stand-
ardise the coinage of the whole Greek
world for the first time. The main currency was the stater in gold and the tetradrachm in silver. The obverse here shows
the head of Hercules, the mythical

forebear of the Macedonian dynasty,
in a lion scalp. His face has distinctly
portrait-like features. On the reverse are
the picture of Zeus enthroned with
an eagle and sceptre, the name of
Alexander and various ancillary marks.

OCTODRACHM

Egypt, Arsinoe II
Philadelphos
Gold, 27.80 g, diameter 27 mm
Inv. No. MK 23.662

Alexander's successors in the various
parts of the Greek world issued coins
with their portraits. This applied also to
the Macedonian Ptolemy dynasty of
Egypt, who brought out really sumptuous pieces of very precious metal in
commemorative issues, like the one
Ptolemy II issued for his wife and sister

Arsinoe II (285–246 BC). The head of the
queen on the obverse of the octodrachm
stands out not just as an outstanding
portrait but also for the delight in detail
and especially the high relief.
The reverse shows a double cornucopia.
Arsinoe is named in the inscription here.

TETRADRACHM

Attica, Athens, 168–167 BC
Silver, 16.77 g,
diameter 31 mm
Inv. No. MK 35.263

The coins of Athens from the late sixth century BC onwards carry the head of the city patroness Athena on the obverse and her emblem, the owl, on the reverse. After a break in minting in the third century following the Macedonian occupation, Athens only began to issue 'new style' coins again from 196 BC.

The obverse of the tetradrachm shows the helmeted head of Athena Parthenos on the right. On the reverse is an owl in a laurel wreath over a reclining amphora, and to the left of it a club and quiver. The inscription names the city of Athens and municipal officials.

AUREUS

Rome, Augustus; minted in
Spain, 19 BC
Gold, 7.81 g, diameter 19 mm
Inv. No. MK 4.632

After the failure of Caesar's attempt, the first Roman emperor, Augustus (27 BC – 14 AD) was more successful at installing a monarchy. His political skills are reflected quite clearly in his coinage, where he contrasts the new with the traditional, as this coin minted in Spain demonstrates. The obverse simply states his titles "CAESAR AUGUSTUS", and shows

a slightly idealised head. The reverse carries the legend "IOV TON (Iov[i] Ton[anti]", i.e. Jupiter the Thunderer) on either side of a six-column temple façade with the image of Jupiter.

TETRADRACHM

Celts, Noricum, Adnamatus,
1st century BC
Silver, 9.9 g, diameter 22 mm
Inv. No. MK 26.732

Celtic coins started out by imitating Greek original mintings, particularly those of the Macedonian kings, though the imitations became steadily more confused. The kingdom of Noricum (centred in present-day Carinthia) struck silver coins large and small, and for a while the names of kings (e.g. "ECCAIO",

"SUICCA" and the like) appeared on the large ones. The obverse of this tetradrachm carries a garlanded male head, the reverse a mounted spearman galloping towards the right. Below in the exergue, the king ("ADNAMAT") is named.

AUREUS

Rome, Septimius Severus,
193–194 AD
Gold, 7.05 g, diameter 21 mm
Inv. No. MK 14.129

Septimius Severus (193–211 AD) was governor of Upper Pannonia in Carnuntum at the time Emperor Commodus was murdered, and it was there that the legion he commanded, the fourteenth, proclaimed him emperor. He was the first of a series of soldier emperors. The obverse of the aureus has the head of the emperor crowned with a laurel wreath with the imperial name, while on the reverse the Fourteenth Legion is named ("LEG XIIII GEM M V [legio XIV Gemina Martia Victrix]"). The two standards of the legion are separated by a legionary eagle.

DENARIUS

Kingdom of the Franks,
Charlemagne; mint: Mainz (?)
Silver, 1.12 g, diameter 17 mm
Inv. No. MK 165.636

King Pippin the Short abolished the double currency of gold and silver coins in the Frankish kingdom. After 755 only a silver coin, the denarius, was minted. Charlemagne (768–814) gradually increased the weight of the denarii, so that finally 240 of them made a Carolingian pound. All old coins were withdrawn. The new coins bearing the monogram of the king were intended to be equally valid wherever they were minted and to be accepted by everyone. The denarius – later called penny – carries Charlemagne's name on the obverse: "CARO/LUSC∽". On the reverse it says "KD/MAG/C", naming the mint.

BRACTEATE
(HOLLOW PENNY)

Halberstadt, Bishop Ulrich von Reinstein
Silver, 0.87 g, diameter 31 mm
Inv. No. MK 214.988

The second half of the twelfth century was the high point artistically and technically in the career of bracteates. Among the many pieces, there are splendid examples of Romanesque miniature engraving, like this bracteate of the diocese of Halberstadt under Bishop Ulrich von Reinstein (1149–1160). Halberstadt, Quedlinburg Abbey, the lords of Falkenstein and Arnstein and the Counts of Anhalt and their mints formed a southern centre of bracteate mintings, using the rich silver lodes of the Harz. The inscription on the single-sided hollow penny ("S-S STEPH-ANVS-PROTH-OMAR/TIR") refers to St. Stephen, the Catholic Church's protomartyr. He is shown here in a half-hovering, half-kneeling position, with his head to one side gazing heavenwards.

PENNY

Austria, Leopold VI;
mint: Vienna, *c.* 1210/30
Silver, 0.90 g, diameter 20 mm
Inv. No. MK 168.855

The Babenbergers set up their first mint around 1110/20 in Krems. In 1193 or 1194, a mint was set up in Vienna, probably due to the eastwards shift of their territory, the arrival of silver as a ransom for Richard the Lionheart and the Babenberger takeover of Styria in 1192. The pennies *(pfennige),* which generally carry no inscriptions, can only be classified and attributed on the basis of comparing coin troves. The many motifs are drawn from the rich visual vocabulary of the Middle Ages. In this case a panther and an eagle are enclosed in an arch on one side, and a leopard-like lion on the other.

PRAGUE GROSCHEN

Bohemia, Wenceslas II;
mint: Kuttenberg/Kutná Hora
Silver, 3.71 g,
diameter 27 mm
Inv. No. MK 165.004

The falling purchasing power of the penny *(pfennig)* and the need for a larger money supply as a result of growing trade led to the issuing of multiples of pennies. The result was the Venetian *matapan* and French *gros tournois*. In 1300, King Wenceslas II (1278–1305) created the Prague Groschen on the French model. The rich silver mines in Bohemia enabled many coins of this denomination to be made, so that they also circulated in neighbouring countries as well. The minting of Groschens continued until the time of Habsburg emperor Ferdinand I. The image is influenced by the *gros tournois:* around the crown of Wenceslas, the name and title of the king fit into a double-circle inscription. On the back it announces: "GROSSI: PRAGENSES", with the crowned Bohemian lion.

GOLD ANGEL
France, Philip VI, France,
1341
Gold, 6.32 g,
diameter 32 mm
Inv. No. MK 21.551 aα

The gold angel *(ange d'or)* was first minted in 1341 under King Philip VI (1328–1350). It was named after the image on the obverse, showing the archangel Michael standing on the dragon with one hand resting on a shield with three lilies. This is the first depiction of the fleur-de-lys shield on a French coin. The ornamental design on the back shows a flower pattern in a quatrefoil, with four little crowns in the corners, while the legend "XPC VINCIT XPC REGNAT XPC IMPERAT" refers to Christ the victorious ruler. It was retained on French gold coins for many years. The French *ange d'or* is among the great achievements of coinage in mediaeval Europe.

GULDINER (UNCIALIS)
Master engraver: Wenzel Kröndl
Tyrol, Sigmund; mint: Hall, 1486
Silver, 31.94 g, diameter 42 mm
Inv. No. MK 164.828

The main coin used in trading in those days was the gold florin. Tyrol lay astride an important trade route between north and south, and this type of gold coin was minted in Tyrol itself under Sigmund (1439–1490). However, minting gold coins was not profitable because there were no gold resources in the country. Sigmund's chancellor Anthoni vom Ross therefore had the brilliant idea of minting the equivalent of the gold florin in silver, using the country's plentiful silver resources instead. The engraving is a major work of Gothic engraving art. It is also outstanding technically, because a relatively large, thick piece of metal had to be handled.

GULDINER

Austria, Maximilian I; mint: St. Veit, 1518
Silver, 26.63 g, diameter 41 mm
Inv. No. MK 164.261

Maximilian I (1493 – 1519) made a major
contribution to the success of the new
coinage that spread from Tyrol. The first
issues from the Carinthian mint in St. Veit
are dated 1515. The bulk of the mintings
were batzes, half batzes and pennies.
St. Veit florins should be considered as
only for show, since the weight of the
pieces varies too much for real coins.
In the large silver coins issued at the time
by the Carinthian mint, the Gothic style
had already given way to Renaissance
motifs.

THALER

Austria, Leopold I; mint: Vienna, 1670
Silver, 28.60 g, diameter 44 mm
Inv. No. MK 726 bα

The coinage during the reign of
Leopold I (1657–1705) was largely
determined by the measure introduced in 1659 known as the *Münz-
einrichtungswerk,* which created new
kinds of coins that generated greater
profits for the mint at much lower
cost. The wars against the Turks had
triggered off a financial and monetary
crisis generally known as the *kleine
Kipperzeit.* This Viennese thaler is an
example of a fine Baroque coin still
short of a perfect finish. Every mint
still had its individual artistic and
technical characteristics.

DUCATON

Master engraver: Jacques Roettiers
Austria, Maria Theresia; mint: Bruges, 1754
Silver, 33.12 g; diameter 41 mm
Inv. No. MK 170.760

In 1714, the War of the Spanish Succession came to an end with the Peace of Rastatt. One consequence was that the Habsburgs acquired the Spanish Netherlands. The ducaton, introduced there in 1618, was supposed to be the silver equivalent of the ducat. It was one of the highest-value silver coins of its time but was no longer minted after 1755. The engraver, Jacques Roettier, signed his work on the arm of the head and shoulders profile of Maria Theresia (1740–1780). On the reverse are the crowned arms with laurel boughs on the fork of a tree. The small lion below is the mark of the Bruges mint.

DOUBLE ASSOCIATION THALER

Master engraver: obv. Josef Tautenhayn sen., rev. Franz Gaul
Austria, Franz Joseph I; mint: Vienna, 1866
Silver, 36.94 g, diameter 41 mm
Inv. No. MK 129.209

The Convention currency introduced during Maria Theresa's reign in 1753 remained in circulation until 1857, when Austria and Liechtenstein concluded a coinage treaty with the states of the German customs union. Under the treaty, the same coinage (*Vereinsmünzen,* union coinage) was to be minted in all the countries party to the treaty: gold crowns, double thalers and thalers. Because the currencies of the three great currency areas of the former German Empire were intended to be harmonised into a favourable exchange rate system with each other, Austria lowered its monetary standard marginally and designated it as the Austrian currency. The engraver's work is flat and precise. The portrait of Emperor Franz Joseph (1848–1916) was standardised for all mint offices, and the emperor's motto ("MIT VEREINTEN KRAEFTEN") was used

as a perimeter inscription. The *ring milling* technique ensured that the edges were very accurate.

ABBOT ULRICH II MOLITOR MEDAL

Medal-maker: Rafael Ranghieri

1581
Silver cast, partly gilt, 54.21 g,
diameter 53 mm
Inv. No. MK 12.818 bβ

Ranghieri must have come to Austria
in the 1560s. He and Antonio Abondio
represented the Italian style of Austrian
medal-making in Vienna and Prague.
Their medals are outstanding for
their portraiture and fine engraving.
This medal shows Ulrich Molitor
(1526–1585), abbot of Heiligenkreuz,
at the age of 55. Originally from
Überlingen on Lake Constance, he
was elected abbot in 1558, having
entered the Cistercian abbey in 1548.
Under his management, the economic
decline of the abbey was arrested.

MEDAL COMMEMORATING THE DANISH VICTORY IN THE BATTLE OF KØGE BAY

Master engraver: Christoph Schneider

1677
Gold, 1258.8 g, diameter 128 mm
Inv. No. MK 249 bβ

This medal is in unusually high relief
for a punched medal, and is a considerable technical achievement. Probably of
German origin, medal-maker Christoph
Schneider worked as a die-engraver in
Copenhagen. Thanks to the contrast
between the three-dimensional rendering of the ships in the foreground and
the flatter engraving in the background,
he created here a strong sense of depth.
He also had a great fondness for detail.
The medal celebrated Denmark's three
naval victories over the enemy Swedish
fleet under King Christian V in 1676 and
1677, particularly the final one in Køge
Bay on 1 July 1677. The Scandinavian
war was a side effect of the hostilities
between France and Brandenburg, and
was finally brought to an end with the
Peace of Lund in 1679.

times, it could be decorated with a precious metal frame and precious stones. The various classes were made from different medals and in different sizes.

In Maria Theresia's day, there were three sizes of oval shape, but later a circular shape became standard. The present Grace medal is of the first size weighing five *lot*. The die was engraved by Matthäus Donner, brother of the famous sculptor Raphael Donner, who in his own field matched him for quality.

As was usual, the Grace medal has the portrait of the monarch on the obverse, with the title in the circumscription. As the medal was struck pre-1745, Maria Theresia is described only as the daughter of Emperor Charles, but she is also mentioned as the Queen of Hungary and Bohemia and Archduchess of Austria.

The reverse bears the motto and device of Maria Theresia. It is made up of emblems for the provinces of Austria, with the lion of Bohemia and the patriarchal cross taken from the arms of Hungary.

MARIA THERESIA GRACE MEDAL

Master engraver: Matthäus Donner
1743
Silver, 87.65 g, oval 68/60 mm
Inv. No. MK 1.853 bβ

Like orders today, the Grace medal was conferred by kings and princes as a decoration or for services rendered. In earlier times, it was often cast, but from Emperor Charles VI's day the Grace medal was die-made in Austria. It was made of precious metal, often gold, and awarded together with a chain or ribbon. In earlier

Appendix

Index by Artists

Works by known artists

Index by Inventory Numbers